Lectionary Reflections

Year B

— ≈ —

Jane Williams

First published in Great Britain in 2005

Society for Promoting Christian Knowledge
36 Causton Street
London SW1P 4ST

British Library Cataloguing-in-Publication Data
A catalogue record for this book is available from the British Library

ISBN 13: 978-0-281-05528-9
ISBN 10: 0-281-05528-9

3 5 7 9 10 8 6 4 2

Typeset by Graphicraft Limited, Hong Kong
Printed in Great Britain by Ashford Colour Press

Contents

—— ≈ ——

Preface

--- ∾ ---

These pieces originally appeared in the *Church Times* as a regular 'Sunday Readings' column. I am very grateful to Paul Handley, Rachel Boulding and the other staff at the paper for the opportunity and the support they offered. I am not a biblical scholar, and took on the task with some trepidation, but have been encouraged by many generous readers of the *Church Times* to think that these reflections may help preachers and congregations to engage with and enjoy the Sunday lectionary readings assigned for use with *Common Worship*.

Advent

The First Sunday of Advent

Isaiah 64.1–9
1 Corinthians 1.3–9
Mark 13.24–37

A monk comes to his abbot, seeking enlightenment. He questions the abbot eagerly and impatiently, firing questions at him. But the abbot says, 'Just look.' The monk is very disappointed, 'I'm always looking,' he says sulkily. 'No, you're not,' says the abbot. 'In order to look at what is here, you have to be here, and you are mostly somewhere else.' Stories like this abound in monastic literature, and in the sayings of the Desert Fathers and Mothers. This particular one comes from the Benedictine tradition (you can read it in full in Joan Chittister's book, *The Rule of Benedict*).[1]

Advent is a time to start preparing to meet God, and most of the preparatory readings suggest that this is, at best, a sobering prospect and, at worst, a positively terrifying one. So it is terribly tempting to feel that we ought to be very busy, so that God will notice and be pleased. Probably for most of us it actually is a very busy time, whether we want it to be or not. Readings like the ones from Mark and Isaiah add to a general feeling of anxiety. There is something scary coming, and we're not quite sure what to do about it. Our instinct is to imitate Corporal Jones from *Dad's Army* and run around shouting 'Don't panic!' That must surely have been the reaction of Jesus's disciples as they listened to Jesus's description of the coming of the Son of Man. What he is describing is nothing less than cataclysmic, and who is this 'Son of Man'? They suspect that he is Jesus, or closely associated with Jesus, but they would much prefer it if Jesus made that clear. The impersonal way in which he talks about the Son of Man's judgement leaves them uncomfortable and uncertain about what their own position is. Are they among the elect or not?

---

[1] Joan Chittister, *The Rule of Benedict: Insight for the Ages*, Crossroad, 1992.

But then, when Jesus gets on to the practical advice, it is very much like that of the abbot to the impatient monk. 'Look, keep awake, be prepared.' Jesus does not recommend any particular kind of activity or busy-ness, just a tense, watchful preparedness, and a way of looking at the world that sees it as full of signs. This is not an easy skill. It is much easier to look at the world and see it either as meaningless or actually as full of absences – places where God is not present, rather than places where, any moment now, he might be. The people in Isaiah have come to see the world as empty of God. God has withdrawn from them, they complain, so no wonder they sin. This is all God's fault. If only God would behave like God, like he used to in the old days, then the people would believe again. If only he would rain down fire, and make the mountains shake with awe, then of course people would serve him gladly. 'Do something, God!' the people shout, 'Let's have a bit of activity!'

Then, suddenly, in the midst of this rather melodramatic breast-beating and accusing of God, the people see themselves. It is as though someone has suddenly put a mirror in front of them, as they act out their rage and shame and shake their fists at God. And they suddenly realize that they are not in charge of this play, rather God is. They see themselves in this harsh mirror, as Wallace and Gromit-like clay figures, whose very existence is dependent upon God. And with this realization, the mirror fills with the reflection not of themselves, but of God. They remember, suddenly, who this God is, their maker and their father. God has not hidden himself from them, but they have been too busy, being somewhere else, looking at everything but God. They need to learn to look again and see the world full of signs of God's mighty power and approaching presence. Like the disciples waiting for the Son of Man, so with Isaiah's people waiting for the return of God: they cannot be sure that what is to come will be comforting, but they do at least know it will be real and not some illusion.

Only the Corinthians seem to be able to wait for the coming of Christ with anything like complacency. But that's because they have the sense to stay where they are and look at Christ. And what they see is the faithful God who, from our creation onwards, comes to us until we meet him as he is, in Christ.

So Advent is like a period of forced inactivity, where you have no choice but to sit still and look, learning to see the world as it actually is, full of signs, joyful or terrifying, of the coming of God.

The Second Sunday of Advent

—— ≈ ——

Isaiah 40.1–11
2 Peter 3.8–15a
Mark 1.1–8

The trouble is that we think we know the end of the story. We think that this time of waiting that we call Advent is all building up to the joyful time of Christmas. In fact, it can hardly be called a 'time of waiting' at all. The Christmas lights and Christmas decorations often precede Advent, and some people are well into their Christmas shopping. No shocks for us, we know what to expect. When we've celebrated the birth of the baby, everything will get back to normal again until next year.

So who is this strange, hairy man, striding out of the desert, shouting? Doesn't he know that this is a time for the family, not a time for unpleasantness? Why is he shouting about repentance? And he seems to have skipped all the bit about the angels and the shepherds, surely the real point of Christmas, and gone straight on to something about baptism and the Holy Spirit. That's not part of this story, is it? Doesn't that come in some other story, that we're not really very interested in? No thanks, let's get back to the baby.

Isaiah seems to be getting into the mood rather better. At least he's talking about comfort and tenderness. But no, there he goes too, ruining a perfectly nice message. He seems to think we only get to the comfort when we've faced the devastation. He's on about the wilderness as well. What's more, he seems to think that we are sitting in a desert because that's what we have made of our lives. He suggests that we've pulled up our roots, and turned away from our ground, our source of water, which is God. Now we are so weak and dry that we drift about aimlessly. For Isaiah, the coming God is not a sweet little baby that we can coo over and then ignore while we get on with our party. Instead, God is like a breath of fire on the dried grass of our lives. When he breathes on us, all that is left is the wilderness and God. When, at last, we have noticed that there is no life in us, then we will see the beginning of the extra-

4

ordinary transformation of the desert. Where there was the empty waste that we made, there will be paths, heralds, shouting, a huge crowd following the glorious king through the wilderness, and everywhere he goes life springs up, life that is directly dependent upon him, and knows it. The lambs don't go searching around for food, but turn directly to the Lord and are lifted up and fed. Oh yes, comfort and tenderness, all right, but only once we realize there is only one source. All the Christmas presents, tinsel and plastic reindeer are just a wilderness, without the life of God.

So perhaps the birth that comes at the end of Advent is not the end, but the beginning. That would make sense, after all. Most births are the beginning of something. When we have met this strange God at Christmas, then we don't pack everything away until next year, but start the journey with him, watching him grow, finding out what he is like, waiting to see the story unfold. Such a lot of waiting in the Christian story. Each time you get to a point that you think is the end, you find it is actually another beginning. After the birth, the ministry of Jesus, which seems to end at the cross. And then, suddenly, there is another beginning, in the resurrection, and things start up again, and end again, as Jesus ascends. This time, the new beginning is the Christian community, living by the Holy Spirit. The history of the Church's life has been a series of deaths, or near-deaths, and rebirths, each one unexpected and unpredictable.

2 Peter suggests that we should be grateful for this odd way of proceeding, grateful for the fact that each ending is actually another beginning, because each new beginning gives us a little longer before we have to face the final end. 'Be grateful for waiting,' Peter says. 'Stand in your wilderness and start to build a place "where righteousness is at home"' (v. 13). We are still a very long way from that dream. That's why Advent readings always contain the sombre note of warning. You think you want the coming of Christ? Are you sure you know what you are asking for? So make the most of this period of waiting, be grateful for Advent and use it, not just to prepare for the birth of the baby, but also to prepare a world where this baby, righteousness incarnate, will be at home.

The Third Sunday of Advent

—— ∾ ——

Isaiah 61.1–4, 8–11
1 Thessalonians 5.16–24
John 1.6–8, 19–28

So at last, after weeks of foreboding, of warnings that the coming of the Lord is not something to take lightly or to meet with unprepared, now at last the excitement begins to mount.

First of all there is John. You could read his self-description as humble and self-effacing, but I'm not sure that it is. It rings with certainty. John knows exactly what he is and what he is not. He knows that he is a necessary part of God's unfolding plan, the first actor on the stage, the narrator who sets the scene and lets us know what is to come. There is barely suppressed excitement in his voice as he scans the crowd, waiting for the face that he knows he – and only he – will recognize. He does not mind that his work will be eclipsed. He understands the job of the herald, both its importance and that it is necessarily transitory. He has no hesitation in applying the words of scripture to himself. He knows that the prophets foretold his coming, and longed to see what he is about to see. John is hugely content to be where he is and what he is. Any part in God's coming is vital.

As soon as John opens his mouth, he brings with him the whole cloud of prophetic witness to what God has been preparing for so long. And although the readings of the last few weeks have reminded us that not everyone will be pleased to see God, or thrilled by what he has prepared for the world, today's reading from Isaiah is full of joy. It is a joy that John would have recognized and identified with, because it is the joy of the one whose news is for others. The joy of the anointed one is in seeing the faces of the oppressed, the captive, the bereaved as they hear the good news he brings. But even this, enormous as it is, is secondary. The real, uncontainable, wild excitement comes in Isaiah 61.10 and 11. The good news that the anointed one brings is the news that, at last, the earth is to see the full nature and glory of God. Righteousness, salvation, justice

6

and praise spring up all over the earth because now, finally, we see what God is like. Just as a garden cannot help growing what is planted in it, so the world cannot help but respond to the righteousness of God.

Does Thessalonians sound a little tame after Isaiah? It shouldn't. The Thessalonians are enjoying what the prophets longed for and John pointed to. And they know it, or if they don't, it's not Paul's fault. Paul is perfectly clear that joy is the natural condition of Christians, quite independent of the outward circumstances. Joy is the gift of the unquenchable Spirit, whose job it is to keep Christians connected at all times to the life of God, offered in Christ. It is the same bubbling spring of excitement found in John the Baptist and in Isaiah, the welling joy of those who have seen the nature of God, and the unfolding of his work. It is, perhaps, a reflection of the joy of God himself, looking on what he made and seeing its loveliness. Now the things that he has made can look at him, making again, recreating, and marvel at the beauty of the creator.

The Shepherd of Hermas, which was written in the second century and widely read and pondered on for generations, says: 'Put sadness away from you, for truly sadness is the sister of halfheartedness and bitterness . . . he that is sad always does wickedly, first because he makes sad the Holy Spirit that has been given to man for joy, and secondly he works lawlessness, in that he neither prays to God nor gives him thanks.'[1]

He might have been echoing Paul. This joy is not dependent upon prosperity, health, luck or anything external. It is based on the extraordinary gift that God the Spirit gives us, of being part of the life and work of God. So, like most of God's gifts, it has a purpose. In joy, we turn to the world God has made, and we become his heralds. Like John the Baptist, we shout aloud about the coming of Christ, who will bring joy to those who have never experienced it before in the whole of their lives. We shout about the faithfulness of God, creator, redeemer and bringer of joy. How extraordinary that Thessalonians says that the basis of our faithfulness to God is joy, and that to fulfil God's law we need to rejoice at what he has done. Now that really might get us into the Christmas Spirit.

---

[1] *The Shepherd of Hermas*, www.earlychristianwritings.com, Mandate 10.

The Fourth Sunday of Advent

—— ∿ ——

2 Samuel 7.1–11, 16
Romans 16.25–27
Luke 1.26–38

How can we honour God? How can we show our gratitude for what he has done and promise our obedience for the future? Perhaps our offerings sometimes resemble the mauled mouse that the cat brings in and lays lovingly at our feet. You can see pride and joy in the cat's face, the knowledge that she has brought something valuable that she herself desires and so expects us to desire too. Is that what our offerings to God are sometimes like? Certainly David is offering God something out of the fullness of his own heart. At last the Kingdom is safe and settled and David has a home. The shepherd boy from the hills, who has lived an unpredictable and endangered life since first the Lord called him into his service is now a King, living in a proper house. No more tents and caves for him. A home no longer has to be something that you can pack up or leave behind at a moment's notice. This house represents safety, security, the fulfilment of a deep need for David. And so he assumes that God would like a house too.

David's desire to honour God is genuine, and he has thought carefully and lovingly about the best way to do it. But he has got it wrong. There is no anger in God's tone as he speaks to Nathan. You can hear the affectionate laughter in the words. But the simple fact of the matter is that although David's deepest need may be for security, God has no need of that at all. Is there some small, unacknowledged part of David that is actually trying to domesticate God? Does David think that if he builds a home for God he will know where God is and what he is up to? In the previous chapter, we have seen how awesome the ark, the place of God's presence, is and that David has hugely mixed emotions about it. He is both terrified and thrilled by it – quite rightly. So does he hope that a safely housed ark will represent a safely tamed God? If so, he soon learns what we all have to learn, that God cannot be tamed and that recognizing what God wants might mean relearning the deepest desires of our own heart.

Patiently, God explains that it is not our job to make him a home, but his job – indeed his joy – to make this world a home for us. The great work is started at our creation, continued through calling his people away from Egypt and into a new community, and completed when God himself comes and makes a home with us. Patiently, the angel comes to negotiate with Mary for the kind of home that God is making. God, whom the whole world cannot contain, waits quietly while his angel talks to Mary. How gentle the angel is, as they talk. Mary is confused, bewildered, uncomprehending, but not afraid of this, God's messenger. How he must have muted himself so that she can ask what she needs to know.

Mary's one question is such a clue to her nature. She does not demand to know exactly what God is hoping to achieve; she does not ask what it will cost; she does not preen and demand praise because she is the one God is asking. All she asks is, 'Aren't I a bit of a problem? Are you sure I fulfil your requirements?' And when the angel replies, 'It's all taken care of,' then Mary says, 'Fine.'

Such an odd, almost low-key conversation to announce that God is coming to make the world his home, and so to make it our home too. Such sensible, manageable care for Mary, at this stage, putting her in touch with Elizabeth, who is the one person who will understand what has happened.

When David offers to make God a home, God explains that his home has always been with his people. He has gone with them, preparing things for them, making provision for them in ways that they never even noticed. He knows that they long for a home, but perhaps they do not realize that they can have no home without him. All the things that we long for, that we search for throughout the world, throughout our lives – love, security, peace, fulfilment, joy – all of these things are to be found in God, our only real home. So now, God is preparing, as Advent moves towards Christmas, to come to us, in our own place, in what we call 'home' and yet are never quite content with. He will make it, and us, his home, so that we can come to our true home, at last.

Christmas

Christmas Day

——— ~ ———

Isaiah 62.6–12
Titus 3.4–7
Luke 2.1–20

In these verses from Isaiah there is a great sense of subdued excitement, of restlessness, of purposeful movement a little distance away, as the dawn breaks. Actually, this would probably describe almost any household with children, on a Christmas morning. In both cases, it is anticipation that causes this stifled bustle.

In Isaiah, the watchmen who have been on night shift, straining their eyes in the dark, whispering to each other about what it is they are looking for, are about to be relieved. The day shift is coming on duty, but the ones who have been there all night are finding it hard to leave. Wouldn't it be awful if it all happened when they were asleep? Normally, watchmen live in the tension of knowing that if they do not see the slight movements of the enemy approaching, then the whole city will be in terrible danger. But these watchmen are not looking out, anticipating attack. They are waiting for salvation. Their excitement cannot be contained. Day and night they can be heard muttering, 'Come on, come on', and occasionally shouting it aloud, as though their impatience will communicate itself to the one they are waiting for.

All their lives, they have lived in garrison towns, watching all around them for the enemy, stockpiling food and necessities behind the walls, knowing that anything left outside the gates is liable to be forfeited to the enemy. But now, all of that is to change. The gates of the city are to be flung open, so that light and air can stream in. The rubble around the city wall is to be cleared away. You no longer need to try to make it hard to reach the city. Instead, all your efforts go into making it easy to reach, and highly visible. People are beginning to pour in and out, looking around them, laughing, shouting, rejoicing.

And then, the sudden hush, followed by a huge roar of sound. At last the Lord is coming! At last the city is a home, not a fortress. The Lord has come home.

This is the way it should be, when the great and conquering King returns, but Luke tells it another way. He shows us a King, laid in an animal feed trough, visited by shepherds. True, the watchmen – the angels – see him coming and announce it. But they do not tell the whole city, the whole world. Instead, with all their glorious joy, they go with their trumpets and banners to a group of shepherds. And where, in Isaiah, you see the whole town transformed, new buildings, new roads, clean, sparkling, waiting for the crowds to come and welcome the King, in Luke you see the shepherds scuttling along, mystified and stumbling, to see a child.

But perhaps the shepherds deserve more credit. The people crowded into the restored city are in no doubt about when the King arrives. They have the shouts of all the people around them, they have the sight of the King himself in all his magnificence. By the time the shepherds reach the child, the angels have gone, and all they see is a rough crib and a tired mother. But they recognize the King instantly, and straightaway take on their share of the herald's job. Just as the angels told them, so they now tell Mary, and anyone else who will listen, shouting their joy at what God has done.

And what is it that God has done? Both for the jubilant crowds in Isaiah's city, and for the shepherds and for us, God has brought freedom. The people of the city no longer have to live in fear, waiting for the enemy, never knowing which direction he will come from, or what the cost will be. They are free to live in their city as a home, safe and peaceful. They have not won any wars, they have not had to pay for their freedom with the lives of their soldiers. It has been given to them by the Lord. And the same is true for us, Titus tells us. We have done nothing to earn this freedom, and yet it is ours. We had been expecting to live all our lives in fear of the enemy, knowing that we might have to pay a terrible price to be free, a price that we were almost certainly incapable of paying. And suddenly the weight is lifted. We turn, expecting perhaps to be taken as slaves by the conquering King who has defeated our enemy, but instead he says we are his children, his heirs, and he pours his largesse over our uncomprehending heads, the richness of his Spirit, proclaiming that we are the freed children of God.

The First Sunday of Christmas

—— ∾ ——

Isaiah 61.10—62.3
Galatians 4.4–7
Luke 2.15–21

Galatians is one of the most moving of all Paul's epistles. Paul is fighting for his calling in this epistle. The fight is partly for himself, because if he is wrong, and God has not called him to be an apostle to the Gentiles, then his whole life is wasted. But more importantly, it is for his converts, because if Paul has mistaken his vocation, then he has misled all those Gentiles who have given their lives to Christ through Paul's preaching. The argument is passionate, personal and convoluted. There are passages of personal history, interspersed with technical and not always transparent pieces of scriptural analysis. There are calm and carefully reasoned passages, side by side with passages that are almost libellous. But this section in chapter 4 is at the heart of the whole argument.

It is hard for us today to hear the real pain and joy in this passage about sonship, but it speaks powerfully of what Paul has given up, and why. All through his childhood and early adulthood, Paul would have believed that he was special, because of his relationship with God. This relationship was not anything he chose or opted into, but was his right, because he was a Jew. He was one of God's chosen people, an inheritor of the promises made to Abraham and David, automatically 'one of the family'.

Paul was clearly not alone in finding Jesus's preaching deeply threatening to that sense of being right with God. The Gospels show us that many of the religious leaders who met Jesus hated him, and rejected all that he said and demonstrated about God. Paul's own rejection of Jesus led him to help in a violent persecution of Jesus's followers, which only ended with his meeting with the risen Lord on the road to Damascus. When Paul accepts that his hostility towards Christians is a hostility towards God, he steps instantly out of his privileged insider's relationship with God.

14

So when, here in Galatians, he talks about our 'adoption' as God's children, there is a complicated and moving dynamic going on. Once, Paul would have assumed that he was a child of God, and heir to God's promises, simply because of who he was and where he was born. But now he accepts in gratitude from God's hands what he once thought was his by right. Yes, he says, we *are* children of God, but only because God chooses us, adopts us and makes us his own. We do not have any automatic right to call God 'Father', but God the Holy Spirit, in his mercy, comes to us, and teaches us how to be children of God. By ourselves, we do not even know the words that describe the relationship. Only God knows what this profound thing, 'sonship', is and only he can teach us its words and its meaning. What Paul preaches to the Gentiles is what he has learned himself, the hard way: you *can* be a child of God, but only if you accept it in gratitude, from God's own hand. If you think you already are a child of God, or that you don't need any teaching about how to be a child of God, or that God is bound to choose you as his child and reject others, then you have not begun to understand what only the Holy Spirit can teach.

Paul saw, in humility and joy, the huge shift that happens when God sends his only Son. Paul saw that all other relationships based on 'rights' have to be reworked, in the light of this relationship that we are offered, to which we respond in gratitude and obedience, or not at all. Mary begins to see it too. Mary watches the strange men who arrive at her son's cradle and demand a part in his birth. She listens as they shout about the child, telling everyone how special he is, boasting about how God sent messengers to them, explaining it all.

'But I thought God's messenger and God's meaning was a gift to *me*,' Mary thought, 'and now I find he has been telling half the world.' Before Mary has even started to be able to cling, to possess, to believe herself the only 'favoured one', the only one capable of helping God and interpreting God, already God begins to loosen her gripping fingers, and teach her that she must share what she has, or lose it. Quietly, 'treasuring these words and pondering them in her heart', Mary names her son. No family names, no names that make him part of her history or Joseph's, but the name the angelic messenger gave her. God does not belong even to us, who love him, and yet he is a gift that we can share.

The Second Sunday of Christmas

—— ∾ ——

Jeremiah 31.7–14
Ephesians 1.3–14
John 1.1–18

At the heart of the Christian proclamation of God is the belief that before time, before creation, before the existence of anything but God, God is already love. God's very nature is the love that flows out and returns, that gives and receives, that multiplies and unites. God is generosity and delight so overflowing that it wishes to share its perfect joy with others. The first stage of this sharing is the creation of the world. John's Gospel radically restates the original biblical creation story in the light of the experience of Christ. We now know, John says, that that outgoing, creating, generating force that unleashes the world in the first place is the Son, the Word of God. The Son channels God's generous, overflowing love outward into the world.

But that is just the first stage. It is not in God's nature to make the world just as a kind of plaything, to be observed with detached amusement. Within his own nature, God knows the pleasure of union, of being together, of complete sharing. And that is what God wills for what he has made. He creates in order to share himself with what he has created. So the next stage is for God to give himself to his creation. Just as it is the Son who gives expression to creation in the first place, so it is the Son who goes out to bring creation home again. The Son brings God into the world that God has made, so that we can look at him and begin to long to share what we see.

'Come,' the Son calls. 'Come and enjoy the love of God, as I do. Come and express the generosity of God, as I do, come and display the glory of God, as I do. Come and be children of God, at home in God, resembling him in every way.'

What an offer. In Jeremiah, the people summon up the last remnants of their strength, and come stumbling and weeping towards this hope. They come from their isolation, terror, poverty, sickness, into God's family. 'I will be your father,' God says to them. 'From now on, I will protect you and provide for you. You are no longer alone.' With incredulous joy, the people turn to God. Some dance and shout and sing, and some sit down, with their arms around each other, and experience safety and love for the first time. They are God's children, sharing all that God has. This is what they were made for, this is reality. All that has gone before is just a bad fantasy.

'That's right,' agrees Ephesians. 'This is what everything is for. God doesn't suddenly have a bright idea and think, "Today I'll adopt a few of those strange humans I made ages ago."' He makes us in order to share himself with us. Subtly, almost teasingly, the image of the Son is the template. 'I wonder when they'll notice,' God laughs to himself. 'I wonder when they'll realize that they are designed to fit?' Carefully, painfully, God works away at the encrusted dirt, the broken and torn limbs, the smashed faces of the creation. Everything that disguises the likeness between us and the Son is washed away until we, even we, can see what we are. But we are very weak. Our eyesight is not good. We look from our renewed selves to the glorious Son and we keep thinking that we must be imagining it. So the Holy Spirit puts God's trademark on us. 'Don't doubt, don't panic, don't worry,' the Holy Spirit says. 'Keep looking at me, and you will see the Son in yourselves more and more. You are children of God, you really are. You were made to share all that the Son is and has.'

But if we take our eyes off the Spirit, everything begins to blur again. John speaks with bitter irony of a world made by God, in God's likeness, through God's love and providence, in which God himself can go unrecognized. Busily, desperately, like lost children, we go running around in panicky circles, hoping to catch a glimpse of that desired and beloved figure. Stand still, John suggests, and look at the Son. You will never find God if you look anywhere else. As you look, the images will gradually coalesce. Through the Son you will see the Father, through the Spirit you will see the Son, through the Father you will see what you are meant to be – made in the image of the Son, to share in God's love and delight. God has made it as clear as he can, coming to live with us, sharing our life, so that we can share the life of the Father's only Son.

Epiphany

The Baptism of Christ
(The First Sunday of Epiphany)

————— ⟋ —————

Genesis 1.1–5
Acts 19.1–7
Mark 1.4–11

What is nothingness? We have no concept of it. Our image of it consists of the absence of things that we can picture and describe, which is very different from the nothingness before creation. Genesis struggles for the words to describe non-existence – 'formless', 'void', 'dark'. Although no words can actually describe nothing, Genesis is trying to convey a powerful sense of absence. Without God, there is *nothing*. Into this nothingness, God comes, and then there is, at once, something describable. God comes as wind, or breath, or Spirit, depending how you translate it, and before he does anything else, he speaks. 'Let there be light,' he says. At once, God begins to make sense out of the world. He begins to make it intelligible, imaginable, by using language. God brings the world out of nothingness into the light, speaking to it and making it part of his own language, his own communication. God talks to the world, as a mother talks to the unborn or newborn child, long before it can possibly understand what is said, because the act of talking signs the new child as part of the human community. So God's act of speech to his newborn world brings it into community with him and marks it, from the start, as destined to be part of God's family.

Just as at creation, so at Jesus's baptism: the Spirit, breath, or wind of God comes down to signal the presence of God and the promise of community with him. Just as at creation, so at this baptism: God's presence begins to make things imaginable, to build sense, to create images. Those watching see an ordinary man go down into the water, to receive baptism, as many others have before. But as Jesus comes out of the darkness of the river, into the light, we see the one whom God loves, and through whom he shares

20

his love with us. God's creating word, spoken at the dawn of the world, is spoken again, to draw us into his community. God's first act, at creation, is to create light, that symbol of understanding and clarity, that makes the world immediately intelligible. The beginning of the new creation is a new kind of symbol. We who have forgotten why the world was made – for loving communion with its maker – are given a new sign. God looks on the new creation, emerging out of the waters into the light, just like the first creation, and says to it, 'I love you.'

At the first creation, the Spirit is the intelligent, image-forming love of God at work. In the new creation in Christ, the Spirit makes the image even clearer. 'Perhaps you have forgotten,' the Spirit says, 'perhaps those first words God whispered into the world have been overlaid with other sounds, and you no longer remember the language of your making. So now, hear it again. God is speaking his Word, loud and clear, in flesh, living with you. This is the community that you belong to, the language you were born to understand, the language of God's love for the world, now shown to you again in the Son.' 'You are mine, I love you, you give me pleasure,' God speaks into the world, making and remaking it.

We plod through our lives, trying to live them as though they are bearable without those words of God. But without the words that give birth to the world, there is no point in it at all. If God does not love us and delight in us, we are pointless. There is no sense at all, in Acts, that the people Paul meets in Ephesus are doing anything wrong. They are earnest, well-intentioned, eager to be baptized and repent. But they don't know what they exist for. They know that they have sinned and must seek forgiveness, and then wait. That is what John the Baptist said, and that is what they have been doing. Paul knows instantly that they are still waiting to hear the Word of God, the word that brings the new life to creation. Repentance is necessary, but it is not the end in itself. We are made to hear God's Word, spoken to us in creation and redemption, the word of love that draws us into the world God has made, the real world, of light and image. God's Word instantly gives us a language, a home, a community. We hear it for the first time at our baptism, and yet it is as familiar to us as the long-forgotten voice of our mother, speaking to us in the womb. This is reality, light and love. This is God, Father, Son and Holy Spirit.

The Second Sunday of Epiphany

———— ∽ ————

1 Samuel 3.1–10
Revelation 5.1–10
John 1.43–51

The beginning of chapter 3 of 1 Samuel says, in a very matter-of-fact way, 'the word of the Lord was rare in those days.' 1 Samuel has already begun to paint a picture – centred round Eli and the once-famous shrine at Shiloh – of a society that does not automatically expect the presence of God. For example, when in chapter 1 Eli first meets Hannah, he does not immediately recognize the intensity of her expression as prayer. The fact that Eli assumes that Hannah has come to the shrine to drink rather than pray suggests what Eli's general experience has been. On the whole, apparently, he has not been used to people coming in off the streets to fall on their knees before the Lord. He has come to expect that the shrine will be used as a shelter from the sun, a place to sleep off a good party, or a place from which his sons will run their rackets. Eli does not expect people to turn to the shrine to seek the word of the Lord.

Eli almost certainly inherited his priestly role, as his sons are doing. They treat the temple at Shiloh as the family business, rather than any kind of vocation. But Eli, at least, has some vestiges of his training that rise to the surface under pressure. As soon as he is forced to recognize Hannah's real need, he responds, perhaps a little blandly and impersonally, but with the correct kind of priestly things. Almost certainly, that is the last he expects to hear of the matter. But again, when Hannah returns a few years later and expects Eli to remember, he knows how to react. To Hannah, at least, Eli's words were the words of the Lord that began the great change in her life.

And now things begin to gather pace for Eli. Casually, without really thinking about it, he invoked the name and power of the Lord for Hannah, and now the word of the Lord is streaming through that tiny, dry channel. In chapter 2, another 'man of God' comes to Eli with a message, and then, in chapter 3, the message is repeated, through Samuel. There must be some part of Eli that longs for the old days, when the Lord kept quiet, and he didn't have to face the reality of the degradation that he and his sons have brought upon their profession and their family shrine. Even when he begins to suspect that Samuel is hearing the voice of God, Eli does not choose to go and wait with Samuel, in the hope that he too might hear the God whom, in theory, he has served all his life. Instead, Eli sends Samuel back alone, while he pulls the blankets up over his head. But at least Eli does not for one moment disbelieve the message of God. He knows its justice, and acknowledges that the judgement of God is true. He may not have heard the word of the Lord himself, but he does recognize it.

So we get the impression of Eli as a man, not wholly bad, but forgetful of his duty to the Lord. Although he is sorrowful and realistic about his sons, he does not send them away, or stop them ministering at Shiloh and using it as the base for their criminal activities. He has no idea what his perfunctory words of blessing to Hannah will unleash. If occasionally in the past he sat around after dinner and murmured nostalgically about the good old days when the word of the Lord was regularly heard by his people, he will soon live to see that the word of the Lord is not a safe plaything, or a nice merit award, but the terrible, dangerous proclamation of the justice of God.

Nathanael, too, will learn that the hard way. When he first meets Jesus, he is looking for a thrill. He is very prepared to find Jesus exciting, and to see everything he does as rather magical. We are not told how he responds to Jesus's drily deflating words or if and when he ever comes to understand the reference to Jesus as the ladder of the angels. When Nathanael runs eagerly up to Jesus, he has no idea at all about how God will choose to bring heaven and earth back into unity through the Son of Man.

The author of Revelation knows, of course. He recognizes the figure of the slaughtered Lamb, despite the fact that it has seven horns and seven eyes. But if he knows the cost of God's justice, still he longs for the time when the Word of the Lord, in all its terror and majesty, will be heard throughout the world.

The Third Sunday of Epiphany

—— ~ ——

Genesis 14.17–20
Revelation 19.6–10
John 2.1–11

We are created to praise God. We cannot truly find our existence in any other way, and neither can the created world, which longs to re-echo to the sound of human voices raised in songs of praise to their creator. So what Revelation is describing is the culmination of all the thousands of words that have gone before it in the Bible. It is describing the world shouting out in love, joy and praise.

In verse 5, a great voice issues from the throne, commanding God's servants to praise him. This is a command that God's people throughout the ages have tried to respond to as faithfully as possible. As the voice from the throne rings out, what sound do we expect to hear? Perhaps the reedy, distant voices of the small congregation somewhere near the back of the church. Perhaps the louder, more confident sound of a big, full church that still cannot help hearing the unheeding roar of the traffic outside. The worship of the churches, faithful throughout the centuries, has yet been marked, perhaps, by a sense of hoping against hope, a knowledge that our own fervent praise is met by a deafening silence or, worse, by real obscenity, from so many of God's human creatures. And if we are truthful, even our own praise of our creator has been marred by uncertainty and division, by inertia and weariness.

But now at last, in Revelation, when the call goes out for the world to praise God, the response is overwhelming. The prophet hears the praising voices all around him, far and near, in such quantities and with such volume that he can only describe it in terms of the sound of a huge waterfall or a massive storm. He has no experience of a human sound to match it, so enormous is the noise. All through the centuries, against such apparent odds, God's servants have declared that he is King, but now at last the prophet sees that the whole world acknowledges it. The Church that John has been describing is not one that can see any visible signs in the

24

world around it of God's Kingship, and yet it has remained certain, under persecution, boredom, weariness, that God is indeed to be praised. As John stands, buffeted by the sound of the world roaring in joy to the King, how he must have thought of the small, struggling churches that he cares for, teaches and prays for. Can these little groups of ordinary people really have something to contribute to this mighty, confident Hallelujah? John knows that they can and do. The voices of all God's faithful servants go to make up the glorious sound. Each individual, however apparently insignificant, adds his or her voice. And suddenly this is not just a huge, joyful chorus in which individuals scarcely matter, and in which the God whom they are praising is, although utterly wonderful, also utterly distant. Instead, the angel comes to John, asking him to deliver wedding invitations to all God's personal friends. 'Tell them all they are welcome,' he says. 'Tell them that they are friends of God, and they have earned their place at this celebration.' Now the song of praise is not just a duty, not just the inevitable tribute paid by a subject to the King, but a song of beloved friends and family at a party or a wedding. This is our song, the song of God's friends, our duty as well as our joy.

But if we can feel, just for a few moments, the surge of love and joy that John is describing, much more of the time we are like the puzzled guests at the wedding in Cana. We are more than happy to drink the excellent glass of wine that God, in his goodness, has provided for us, but we quickly forget it and often fail to make the connection between this present gift and the duty of gratitude and praise that we owe to God for so much more than just this one moment of joy.

At this wedding, Jesus is the guest, and he adds a dimension of happiness that would otherwise be lacking. So when we are the guests at his wedding feast, what rejoicing we can expect.

Why does John say that this strange and irrelevant miracle 'revealed his glory'? Only Mary and the disciples know what has happened. Does it give them some insight into the kind of God they are serving? All of them will experience suffering, grief and loss as a result of their love of Jesus, but that is not what they were created for. They were created to share in the scene of wild rejoicing that Revelation describes. Drink this wine in remembrance.

The Fourth Sunday of Epiphany

— ◇ —

Deuteronomy 18.15–20
Revelation 12.1–5a
Mark 1.21–28

'If I hear the voice of the Lord my God any more, or ever again see this great fire, I will die' (Deuteronomy 18.16). This, according to Deuteronomy, is the source of prophecy. The people of God have experienced the unmediated presence of God at Horeb, and they know that they cannot bear it again. Although in the garden of Eden Adam and Eve could walk side by side with God and talk to him in the cool of the evening, one of the results of the Fall is the loss of this intimacy. The people are no longer capable of being in the unveiled presence of God. From now on, they need to hear God's Word mediated through other human agencies, rather than direct from the mouth of God.

God shows no disappointment at this request on the part of his people. On the contrary, he acknowledges its justice. They are quite right to think that the presence of God could be fatal to our faulty senses, like a powerful electric current passing through a wrongly wired plug. So God makes alternative provision for his people, since it would be equally fatal for them to attempt to live their lives without hearing God's Word at all. God promises to raise up prophets for them, people who will be capable of receiving God's words and transmitting them faithfully.

But the people have to understand clearly that this is no soft option. They cannot use this as an excuse not to listen to God. They cannot say, 'We are not capable of being in God's presence and hearing his words, so we'll just have to get on with our lives as if he didn't exist.' On the contrary – they have asked for prophets, and they must take their prophets with the utmost seriousness. The whole people must take seriously their responsibility to weigh the words of prophecy and discern where God is genuinely speaking and where he is not. The failure to listen on the part of the people, or the misuse of the Word of God on the part of the prophet, will have equally serious consequences.

But of course the history of God's people, from that day to this, is full of instances of failures to listen and abuses of God's authority. The art of discerning whether or not the word is from God is one that has to be practised with great patience, and we are not a patient people. So by the time the Word of God comes in person, there is almost no tradition by which to measure him or listen to him. John's Gospel spells that out for us in its first chapter. 'He came to what was his own, and his own people did not accept him,' John tells us in 1.11. Mark makes the same point with understated irony. Here in chapter 1 it is only the mad man who recognizes Jesus. It is as though his illness has actually scraped away layers of blindness and insensitivity so that he is aware, as no one else is, of God's presence. Like the Israelites on Horeb, he is terrified by it. When Jesus heals him, there is a bitter irony in realizing that the man is being restored to the normality of the human community around him and, at the same time, losing his ability to discern the fearful presence of God. That is what is 'natural' to us now, not to be able to see God.

The lectionary-makers could have given us a reassuring third reading, reminding us that although we have unfitted ourselves for the presence of God, through our choices and the whole way in which we live our lives, as individuals and as communities, God himself has given us back the gift of discernment, the Holy Spirit. But instead they have given us the strange and frightening reading from Revelation. Perhaps they are right. Perhaps we pass over, too superficially, the terrible cost of our distance from God. Perhaps, too, we are too prone to accept God's self-gift and domesticate it, allowing ourselves to become cosy with God. But the Israelites knew themselves and their God well when they remembered how terrifying they had found it to meet him. Just because God has acted with graciousness and love to come to us and live with us, that does not mean that we should forget who and what he is. Revelation describes the cosmic consequences that follow from our sin and, although it reiterates, again and again, the triumph of God, perhaps it is right that we should remember what kind of a God it is who wins this victory for us.

Ordinary Time

Proper 1

—— ∼ ——

Isaiah 40.21–31
1 Corinthians 9.16–23
Mark 1.29–39

There are two complicated, separate yet related themes running through today's readings. The first is to do with proclamation – all three passages talk about the ways in which God makes himself known to us. The second is to do with the demands of that proclamation. To know God is to relinquish other 'rights' that might conflict with what a relationship with God requires.

Isaiah's understanding of how God is proclaimed is fierce and uncompromising. The whole world – its very existence – shouts out the presence of God. The puny people who run around on the surface of the earth, thinking themselves important, have only to look up at the vastness of all there is and realize their mistake. Even princes and rulers have no more claim to power over God's earth than the grass that grows under their feet. All authority and power belong to God alone. So when God's people start to grumble that God doesn't seem to be paying enough attention to them, they need to remember just who they are and, more importantly, who they are not. God is not at their beck and call, and they cannot demand that he explain himself to them.

The sheer, overwhelming force of the creation's witness to God should remind his people that they do not have any 'rights' in relation to God. If, in his grace and mercy, he chooses to give them gifts, they can never assume that they have deserved these things, or earned them in any way. They cannot insist on having them, like the payment of wages.

Paul agrees with that. It's one thing that does come clearly out of this very complex and opaque passage of 1 Corinthians. Paul is absolutely certain that being a minister of the gospel is not a 'job' for which wages are due. Proclaiming the gospel is simply what he has to do, like breathing. That is not to say that it goes unrewarded, but the reward is the preaching itself – to share with others freely the free gift that he has been given, through the gospel. Paul is no more to be commended for doing this than the creation is. Isaiah does not congratulate the created world on bearing witness to its creator – of course it must.

And just like the creation, Paul is not free to dictate the terms under which he proclaims God's message. He cannot insist that people accept it only in one particular kind of package. It almost sounds as though Paul is saying that he will sink to any kind of subterfuge to make himself acceptable to people, but that is to miss the sense of compulsion in Paul's description of his relationship to his calling. He is there to be used by others. Just as the creation has no other purpose than to bear witness to its creator, so Paul has no other purpose than to preach the gospel. He is as freely available to all as the witness of creation is. The Corinthians seem to think that being an Apostle might be a bit of a power trip, or at the very least an easy way to get other people to feed you and pay you, but Paul is trying to explain that to be a minister of the gospel is to be at God's disposal and the disposal of others, and to abandon yourself to the purposes of God.

That sense of the compulsion to preach the gospel is also there in Jesus's ministry. Others would obviously have liked to interpret his calling differently. He could have stayed at Simon Peter's house indefinitely, and all the sick for miles around would have come to him for healing. And surely that would have been a good thing, a ministry worth having? Simon clearly thought so. He was probably rather enjoying the glory of having the healer staying with him. Perhaps the crowd gathered outside his house are asking him to intercede on their behalf, to make sure that Jesus sees them. So when Simon goes looking for Jesus in the early morning, there is a slight sense of impatience in his voice. 'Why are you wasting your time out here in the desert, when there are people who need you?' Simon seems to say.

For answer, Simon gets swept up into the whirlwind of Jesus's real ministry, which is to travel round and talk about God, to any-one and everyone who will listen. That is what he is there for and, very soon, it is what Simon is there for too, as are we. We are bound to proclaim our God, just as the world he made is. We have no other purpose.

Proper 2

———— ∾ ————

2 Kings 5.1–14
1 Corinthians 9.24–27
Mark 1.40–45

Mark's Gospel is almost certainly the oldest of the four Gospels. Matthew and Luke seem to know it and depend upon it for some of their information, though they do also have independent sources of their own. It is possible that, rather than Matthew and Luke having read Mark, all three of these Gospels have an earlier, perhaps un-written, source in common. Scholars usually call this hypothetical Gospel 'Q'. The connections between the first three Gospels are fascinating, and it is always intriguing to read, for example, one of Jesus's parables as relayed in three slightly different forms. Oceans of ink have been expended by New Testament experts on arguing about why Matthew puts a parable in a different context from Luke, or why Luke changes the audience from Mark's version. This is what is called 'the Synoptic Problem', and any good commentary will give you some introduction to the main discussion. (John's tradition, by the way, is strikingly different in a number of ways from the first three Gospels.)

Mark's is the shortest of the Gospels, and its narrative is urgent, spare and driven. Nearly half the Gospel is directly concerned with the events leading up to Jesus's crucifixion. From Mark 8.27, where Peter declares Jesus to be the Messiah, the emphasis is on the prep-aration for death. But held in tension with this concentration on Jesus's fate is Mark's description of Jesus's power. Whether teach-ing, healing or simply moving around among the people, everyone reacts to Jesus. We have already seen how the fishermen give up their livelihood to follow him, how the unclean spirits fear him, how the sick and the desperate mob him wherever he goes. Mark is by no means portraying Jesus as a victim. On the contrary, the way in which he prepares for his death is part of his 'authority' – a word that Mark puts into the mouths of those who meet Jesus, for example in 1.27. Everything Jesus does, from beginning to end, is proclaiming the Kingdom of God, and Mark makes it clear that the way people react to Jesus is the way they react to God's reign. Jesus comes out of the wilderness proclaiming the Kingdom, and at his death the veil of the Temple is torn down, so that nothing protects the people from the direct presence of God again.

But while Mark constantly highlights Jesus's power, he does this by throwing the light on the stunned or angered faces of the audience, so that we cannot miss the effect Jesus is having. But at the same time he puts into Jesus's own mouth words of disclaimer. He wants you to see what Jesus has done, but every time you go to foreclose the discussion about who Jesus is, Mark says, 'Wait, think, there is more.' This is what is usually called the 'messianic secret' in Mark. Jesus seems to turn aside all attempts to identify him with the coming Messiah. But Mark certainly does not allow us to think that that is because Jesus was something less. On the contrary, the whole narrative demands that you ask more and more about Jesus.

But the leper in today's reading is asking no more questions – for the moment. He has the answer he needs, and is sharing it with everyone. He asked the one question he really wanted to ask, 'Can you be bothered with me?' It is not the standard request for help, but a genuine uncertainty about whether anyone could believe he deserved it, and we are told that his words moved Jesus. The other healings we have seen in this chapter do not mention Jesus's emotions, but something about this man's mixture of boldness and uncertainty touches Jesus. The man knows that Jesus is in control of his healing power, and can choose whether to heal or not.

When the healing is complete, Jesus sends the man straight off to register himself with the priest, so that he can be included again among his people. We are told that Jesus is 'stern' in his command that the man say nothing about the source of his healing. But the man cannot obey that command. It is simply beyond him. He is elated and uncontainable in his joy. We do not know quite what he told people, but whatever it was it results in such fame for Jesus that he cannot go into the town any more. Healing brings the leper back into his proper human community, but his witness to Jesus has the opposite effect. Jesus's power is already beginning to be costly, and to set him outside the community to whom he has come to proclaim the Kingdom of God.

Proper 3

———— ⟨⟩ ————

Isaiah 43.18–25
2 Corinthians 1.18–22
Mark 2.1–12

Our capacity to respond wrongly to God is endless. All three of today's readings focus primarily on the generosity of God, but they also all have as a backdrop the stubborn stupidity of our response.

The miracle that Jesus performs in the reading from Mark's Gospel is a much loved story. What Sunday-school child hasn't drawn diagrams of the flat-roofed homes of Jesus's day, to illustrate how the friends of the paralysed man would have been able to lower him down in front of Jesus? And they had to resort to such methods because so many people had come to see and hear Jesus that they couldn't get through any other way. That already starts to make us wonder about the crowd. Jesus already, at this early stage of his ministry, has a reputation as a miracle worker. You might have expected the crowd to make room for the stretcher-bearers to get through, even if only in the hopes of seeing something magical. But no, the crowd are selfishly oblivious to the paralysed man and his need. They have come to see a spectacle, but at heart unconvinced, they are certainly not going to do anything to help Jesus prove himself.

So they are all ready to start arguing, as soon as Jesus begins to talk to the paralysed man, and although they seem temporarily convinced when the man gets up and walks away, we know that this is just the beginning. This group of people, who wouldn't let the man through to Jesus, who disputed Jesus's right to forgive sins, who are appeased for a few moments by something exciting – this group are the ones who will follow Jesus all through the gospel story, vacillating about their reaction to him. And in that respect, they are just like us. Jesus offers forgiveness and healing, and sometimes we think that's wonderful and sometimes we just can't be bothered.

Isaiah, too, has a mixed message for God's people. What God promises is a new start, where all the old bitter history of betrayal and sin is wiped away. The wilderness that the people have made of the promised land will suddenly be fertile and full of the sound of running water. From the dry throats, which had breath only to grumble and curse, will come again the praise for which they were designed. People will drink God's life-giving water and sing out their thanks.

But actually, of course, they don't. They drink the water all right, but the thanks? Instead of praise and gratitude, the people carry on as though this great new thing that God is doing simply hasn't happened at all. They take what they can and forget who has provided it.

The words that Isaiah puts into God's mouth are full of weariness and disappointment. They are the words that we would say if we were God, and they are the words that we should expect, because we have deserved them. But they are not God's own words, according to Paul. God's words to us are never just what we deserve; they are never what we, in our self-righteousness and anger, would say to each other. Instead, what God says to us is 'Yes'. Steadily and faithfully, God says 'Yes' to us, over and over again. Human nature might be changeable, and human plans might mean that a 'Yes' sometimes has to become a 'No', but God is not like that.

Jesus is God's great 'Yes' to us, Paul says. However often we say 'No, we are not God's creatures; No, we do not belong together; No, we don't even believe in God', Jesus simply says 'Yes'. 'Yes, God made you and loves you and shares his life with you and believes in you. Yes.' Jesus's 'Yes' is patient and inexorable. It does not shout down or drown out our 'No', it simply outlasts our feeble voices, so that all that remains is his 'Yes'.

So we need to recognize the fretful and changeable crowds who followed Jesus as ourselves. And we need to look back over the human centuries of avoiding God and his call and feel the weariness of the world at our stupidity. But we must never come to believe that our negative can be stronger than God's 'Yes'. There is a kind of fierce, baffled, shameful pride in thinking of our sins as so great that they can distort the purposes of God. It may take a great deal of humility to understand that even our most resounding 'No' is still only really like a child having a tantrum. God is not the kind of father who gives in to tantrums, because he knows we do not really know what we need. Jesus is what we need, God's great 'Yes'.

The Second Sunday Before Lent

———— ❧ ————

Proverbs 8.1, 22–31
Colossians 1.15–20
John 1.1–14

Recently, a lot of my letters and conversations have been with people who are really struggling to believe in the love of God in the face of personal and impersonal suffering. Some have come through an experience of watching someone die horribly, some have been overwhelmed by the weight of evidence of starvation and brutality from around the world. Some simply look at the world around them and see it primarily in terms of absence, rather than presence. They cannot see signs of an intelligent and loving purpose, rather a completely random and meaningless set of occurrences.

The Sunday lectionary readings do, on the whole, allow us to focus on the central Christian belief that God does all things out of love towards his creation. Even when the readings focus on the suffering of, for example, Paul or the Christian community, this pain is held securely in a circle of belief about its value and meaning. For those who are already so deeply committed to the purposes of God that they see everything, whether good or bad, as part of that, it is sometimes hard to hear the seriousness and indeed the religiousness of this question about God and suffering. Those who ask the question long with passion to see a world in which they could believe in the goodness of God, but they just can't.

Today's readings do affirm the goodness of creation and of its God, but they do so in a way that requires us to take seriously religious questioning. And that is because at the heart of what is being said today is the statement that God's creative intelligence has something about it that we should recognize. Proverbs calls it Wisdom, John calls it the Word, and John and Paul both call it Jesus. Jesus is the language in which the Creator speaks to us, a language which we at least partly know, and which we can learn if we try, with a lot of help.

Proverbs speaks of Wisdom as sharing in making creation habitable for people. As God measures things, as he makes the earth firm and confines the sea, as he creates water and fixes up the sky, there beside him is Wisdom, working with him. Together they plan all the delightful treats they have in store for their new creation. God looks at Wisdom and thinks, 'Soon there will be others to share in this, as Wisdom does.' Wisdom looks at God and thinks, 'Soon there will be others who will understand and love God's wonderful ideas, as I do.'

John, too, describes God's creative work as being shaped in a way that is, in principle, comprehensible to us. God speaks the Word, and the Word is, by definition, a means of communication. Indeed, it is one of the characteristics of human beings. For John, God's whole purpose, from beginning to end, is to communicate with us and allow us to begin to enter into that communication, begin to learn to speak God's Word. But John introduces a cautionary note, which is also bitterly ironic. God speaks to us in a language that we were designed to understand, and comes to us in a form that is utterly familiar to us, and yet some of us still manage not to recognize him. John can only see the stupidity and waste of those who cannot hear when God speaks to them in their own language.

Colossians, too, is aware that not everyone has seen what God is doing through Christ, in creation and redemption. But in today's passage, we have the stunning image of the ongoing synthesizing work of God. God reaches out to his estranged creation, to bring it back into communication with him, to re-establish the language that allows us to see the purposes of God.

So when we call out to God in anger at so much evil and suffering, we are demanding that God explain the world to us, as he himself seems to promise he will, by creation through 'Wisdom', 'the Word', 'the image of the invisible God'. We are demanding that God be God. God's answer is the Word, Jesus. It is, in one sense, no answer because it does not take away the suffering and injustice that we cannot bear to see in God's world. But Jesus suggests God's anger and love in the face of suffering. He also suggests a way of living that confronts injustice, that has compassion for suffering, that brings the vitality of God into everything. And he suggests a way of dying that might hold, contain and transform evil and suffering.

Is that enough? If not, honour God by demanding to see the 'image of the invisible God', through whom all things have been created and who makes God known to us.

The Sunday Next Before Lent

———— ✑ ————

2 Kings 2.1–12
2 Corinthians 4.3–6
Mark 9.2–9

Elijah is taking part in his own funeral procession. Everywhere he goes, people come out to watch him, the coffin, go past. The people do not speak to him. It's almost as though they think that he has already lost the power of speech and hearing. They talk instead to Elisha, the next of kin, checking how he is feeling about his impending bereavement, but also, of course, pointing out their credentials as prophets. Prophets are supposed to know this kind of thing, and could certainly never hold their heads up again if they could not predict the death of Elijah, the Father of all the prophets. They slightly hope that they are telling that upstart, Elisha, something he didn't know. But no such luck. And he's quite rude to them, basically telling them to shut up when they try to talk to him.

What is Elisha feeling? The prophets are treating him like Elijah's servant. That's certainly what they call him, and they seem determined to demonstrate their own prophetic powers, as though to point out the fact that Elisha was just a ploughman before Elijah inexplicably called him into service (see 1 Kings 19.19f. for the story). They are adding to the great feeling of uncertainty that is filling Elisha as he doggedly follows his master. Elijah isn't really helping. He seems to be trying to get rid of Elisha, constantly suggesting that he might like to stay behind, first saying he's just going to Bethel, then to Jericho, then to the Jordan. If Elisha had waited in Gilgal, as Elijah originally suggested, he wouldn't even have known where his master was when the Lord took him. Elisha has given up his family and his livelihood to follow Elijah, and he has, at present, no idea of what will happen to him when Elijah is taken away.

But his faith is to be rewarded. At last he is alone with Elijah on the other side of the river, and at last Elijah turns to him. When Elijah asks what Elisha wants, the answer comes out so slickly that it's clear Elisha has been thinking it over for some time. He wants to be a prophet of the Lord and he wants to be not just as good, but better than his master.

The vision that he sees is one that reinforces his belief in the importance of the prophet. All the chariots and horsemen of Israel come to meet Elijah, and Elisha is overwhelmed. What's more, although he may not be able to take it in at the time, the vision is entirely for his benefit. No one else witnesses it. It is a gift for him, a confirmation of his calling. When Elisha returns to the other prophets, no one is in any doubt about the fact that he is Elijah's successor.

Is this the function served by the Transfiguration? Is it a confirmation for Peter, James and John of their calling? They are the only witnesses to the extraordinary sight of Moses and Elijah deferring to Jesus. They hear God's voice, telling them that Jesus speaks for him. What wonderful assurance for these men who have given up everything to follow Jesus.

Well, perhaps it would have been if Jesus himself didn't keep confusing the issue. Peter must be tempted to turn to Jesus and say, 'See, I told you you were the Messiah. Why won't you let us tell everyone else what we now know for sure?' But the problem is, that although God has now left them in no doubt about who Jesus is, he has also said that they are to listen to Jesus, and Jesus has just been explaining to them exactly how he sees his own calling. Both before and after the Transfiguration, Jesus talks about suffering and death. How are the disciples to put together what they have just seen and what Jesus is telling them? How are they to be faithful to the vision and the command of God, which seem to point in different directions? The vision tells them how important Jesus is, and the command tells them to listen to him while he stresses how he must suffer and die.

Poor disciples. How they must have envied Elisha, picking up his mantle of power in the certainty of his calling. All they can now be certain about is that they must follow Jesus and, somehow or other, try to hear his baffling words as the words of God. Paul would sympathize with them. He knows that Jesus's gospel is still 'baffling' to many, but nothing will prevent him from preaching it. He is going to proclaim Jesus and trust to God to do the rest.

Lent

The First Sunday of Lent

—— ✌ ——

Genesis 9.8–17
1 Peter 3.18–22
Mark 1.9–15

When God makes his covenant with creation after the flood, it is a covenant not just with Noah and his family, or even with all future human beings, but with 'every living creature that is with you' (v. 10). What's more, God goes on to emphasize this, by detailing all the creatures who are to be involved in this new covenant. Every time the covenant is mentioned, the living creatures are deliberately included (see Genesis 9.12, 15, 16, 17). It is as though Noah's action then binds human and animal destiny together for ever.

But, of course, Genesis has already suggested, in its first creation story, that that was always God's intention. When God makes human beings in chapter 1, he does so expressly saying that human beings are to be responsible for 'every creeping thing that creeps upon the earth' (Genesis 1.26). According to Genesis, human beings have always been closely bound up with the rest of the created order, so when Noah takes animals into the ark to preserve them, he is exercising the proper stewardship for which people were created. It is his duty and his joy to care for what God has made. So when God tells Noah that the new covenant is to include the rest of creation too, God could not have paid him a higher compliment. 'Thank you, Noah,' he is saying, 'You are helping the world to be the way it should be.'

This intimate and necessary connection between the human creation and the rest of what God has made is part of what Lent is supposed to help us rediscover. So much of our human lives is constructed around the premise that we can isolate and protect ourselves from the forces that beset the rest of the world. We build houses to shield ourselves from the elements, we generate electricity to keep out the dark and make night and day bend to our will, we develop medicines to keep death at bay – the list is endless. And when the forces of nature break through and we have to submit to them, we are outraged.

Lent challenges us to remove some of our safety nets. Most of us do that in very small ways. We give up alcohol, or chocolate or (my own vice) coffee, and it is frightening how hard it is to manage without these inessential luxuries. Many human beings, of course, manage daily without such cushions. But Lent is not just an exercise in breast-beating and self-testing. Its basic questions are: 'What are you for?' 'What do you depend on?' 'Where do you get your self-definition?'

The story of Noah is perfectly clear about the proper answers to that. All life is utterly dependent upon God. If God did not choose to preserve it, it would not be. If you depart from that basic fact, then you have lost the possibility of finding out your purpose.

The first three Gospels all bear witness to a turning point in Jesus's ministry, where he had to go into the desert to find out what he was for. Matthew and Luke spell this out quite compellingly. (John, as so often, has a different pattern entirely, and does not mention the wilderness experience.) Mark is, as usual, brief to the point of curtness. But this Gospel does include a detail that the other two do not. Mark says that Jesus was 'with the wild beasts'. At his baptism, God speaks with a love that is to compel everything that follows in Jesus's ministry, and Jesus's response is to go into the desert, with the wild beasts. I do not wish to romanticize animals. It may be that Mark only wants us to see Jesus's vulnerability. But it is tempting to see more in this phrase. It is tempting to read it in the context of the stories of Creation and Flood, and to see Jesus accepting his destiny as the one who is to fulfil the Creator's intention. The wild beasts do not try to protect themselves from God, or from the effects of our Fall. They accept death and disease, and they do not fight against their mortality. It is as though they are one kind of paradigm of acceptance. They accept that they have no control over their fate.

But Jesus is another kind of paradigm. He too is about to accept his part, and to relinquish control, so as to acknowledge dependence upon God alone. But his is the acceptance that is to bring God and humanity together again, as at the beginning.

Our Lenten discipline cannot bring us back to Adam's state, or even Noah's, but it can help us to accept, with gratitude, our creation and re-creation in Christ.

The Second Sunday of Lent

—— ❧ ——

Genesis 17.1–7, 15, 16
Romans 4.13–25
Mark 8.31–38

The Old Testament readings for Lent this year are encouraging us to think about covenants. Last week we had the covenant with Noah, this week we have Abraham, and next week – let me give you a sneak preview – we get the Ten Commandments. On a superficial reading, covenants are a good choice for Lent, because they remind us about obligations, about promises made between two parties, about duty. But actually, both the covenant with Noah and the one with Abraham seem to undermine that serious, disciplined note, because it is not until we come on to next week's reading that we start to hear about our side of the bargain – be sure not to miss next week's thrilling episode.

But as God speaks both to Noah and to Abraham, the duties are all on one side – God's. God promises huge things to both of them, and asks almost nothing in return. In verse 1 of today's reading from Genesis 17, Abraham is told to walk before God 'and be blameless', but there is no suggestion in the promise that follows that the covenant is dependent upon Abraham's behaviour. The command to 'walk blameless' is not attached to the promises but to God's statement about himself. 'I am God Almighty. Walk before me and be blameless.' Both Abraham's status and the fulfilment of the promises being made are wholly dependent upon the nature of God, not upon Abraham.

This is certainly the interpretation that Paul puts upon the matter. He is absolutely clear that Abraham does not receive from God because he has kept his side of the bargain and God must do the same. Abraham has not earned the fulfilment of God's promise, and it is not dependent upon him. The promise to Abraham is fulfilled because the one who makes the promise is God, 'who gives life to the dead and calls into existence the things that do not exist' (Romans 4.17). It is the nature of God the giver that guarantees the

44

gift, not the nature or acts of Abraham, the receiver. The only thing Abraham does is to recognize what God is like and trust him to be able to fulfil the promises he makes.

God's covenant with Abraham comes as a series of steps, all of them leading Abraham into a deeper and deeper exploration of the trustworthiness of God. And, of course, he can only test God's trustworthiness by trusting. By the time we come to chapter 17, Abraham has already left his homeland and been through a great many vicissitudes, following God's command, and so far he has more reason to trust than to distrust. He is alive, well and prosperous. But the thing that set Abraham off on this great adventure was actually not a desire for God, or even wealth, but a longing for a son. And although God has been hinting at this all along (see 12.2, 13.16, 15.4), he has yet to deliver on this promise. In fact, by chapter 16 Abraham and Sarah have decided to take matters into their own hands, and bypass God.

This covenant in chapter 17 marks a new phase, which is symbolized by a change of name for both Abraham and Sarah (see 17.5, 15). The journey so far has led them a long way into trusting God, but now they are to see that God is to be trusted beyond their wildest dreams. And just as the covenant with Noah is both a fulfilment of what God promised Noah and a promise for the rest of the world, so is the covenant with Abraham. Abraham and Sarah are to have the child that they long for, but they are also to be 'ancestors of a multitude of nations' in a way that they could never have anticipated. Paul spells it out for us – God's promise to Abraham is a promise to us all.

Lent is a good time for taking small steps in trusting God, and these steps are not about making ourselves feel better and holier, but about allowing ourselves to explore the trustworthiness of God. But the reading from Mark does sound a necessary sombre note. You will only find God trustworthy if you want what God is offering. Abraham could trust because he wanted a son more than comfort or safety. Jesus's challenge to his disciples throughout the ages is the same. God's promise to the followers of Jesus is that they, like Abraham, will have the chance to be parents to millions, bringing them into the family and the life of God. If I am honest, that is not my deepest desire. Peter speaks for many of us when he rebukes Jesus's interpretation of God's promise. But he got another chance to learn to trust God for what he is actually promising.

The Third Sunday of Lent

——— ⟶ ———

Exodus 20.1–17
1 Corinthians 1.18–25
John 2.13–22

Are Exodus and 1 Corinthians in direct conflict with each other? Do they give wholly irreconcilable pictures of the nature of God and our response to it? The God of the Ten Commandments is, surely, a God who loves order and rules and rational systems. In order to please this God, we have just to follow his rules. The God of 1 Corinthians, on the other hand, is anarchic and incomprehensible, and the only way of pleasing him is to abandon your own rational concepts of hierarchy and order and preach 'Christ crucified' as the defining picture of God.

At this point in Lent, some of us would like to take the 1 Corinthians reading of the nature of God completely out of its context and allow ourselves to give up on rules and discipline. 'God's not like that,' we tell ourselves, comfortably, as we sip our first glass of wine for a couple of weeks, 'he's interested in grace, not law.' But I'm sorry to have to tell you that there is a strong strand of the Christian ascetical tradition that sees this kind of Lenten discipline as responding precisely to that anarchic and unpredictable streak in God. After all, unless you are really addicted to coffee or wine or chocolate biscuits, there is no particularly sensible reason for giving them up. Lent is simply a time for reminding ourselves that the world may not be quite what it seems. Lent nudges us into thinking about what we are here for, which is more than just living comfortable lives with as little unpleasantness as possible. The desert fathers and mothers of the early Christian centuries went out into the wilderness partly at least as a challenge to the increasing wealth and stability of the cities they left behind. 'Don't forget', their lives shouted, 'that God is unpredictable. We are being fed here in the desert with food far more fitted to our needs than all of the dishes that are spread on your groaning tables.' And if most of us are not called into the desert, all of us need to allow God to surprise us from time to time, by leaving our routines and our comforts behind, at least for a while.

But if you think the Ten Commandments are the other side of God, the safe side that you can get back to when you have dipped your toe adventurously into Lent, think again. The Ten Commandments aim to create a society that can recognize the strange, irrational work of God, and be ready to preach 'Christ crucified'. If we have made them into tame, safe rules it is only because we have a genius for dumbing God down, to the point where we can't hear him too clearly – after all, we manage to wear crucifixes as jewellery.

If you forget what you thought you knew about the Ten Commandments and read them again, it is clear that God is asking something extraordinary of his people. He is asking them to throw away all their other comforts and securities and rely on him alone. He is asking them to forget all the normal rules of power and dominance and build a society that will reflect God's own strange preference for the poor and the powerless. The Israelites are, rightly, terrified. From the top of a mountain wreathed in smoke and fire, too holy even for the priests to approach without the utmost caution, comes this picture of how the people of God should live. Above all, they are to believe that only this God is real and holy. No other back-ups are allowed. You can't believe in God and carry on propitiating other kinds of gods. As the hot ash fell on them, and the thunder deafened them, that may have been obvious to the Israelites, but people are good at forgetting. The rules that follow are equally hard and strange. Why waste one whole day resting? You can't even choose which day, and you can't make your slaves work on that day either, or even give them a different day off. One whole day when you have to remember that the world is not just there for your use. And as if that isn't weird enough, you then have a set of rules designed to prevent people from using their natural advantages to their own ends. The strong cannot take what they want, the clever cannot lie their way out of things, the sexy cannot go off with whoever they fancy.

These commandments are not the rational system anyone would come up with. They are the 'foolishness' of the same God who demonstrates his holy might on the cross. If we have forgotten it, like the moneychangers in the Temple, be reminded by Jesus's reaction.

The Fourth Sunday of Lent

—— ❧ ——

Numbers 21.4–9
Ephesians 2.1–10
John 3.14–21

The imagination nourished by the Bible immediately springs into action at the mention of snakes.

In Numbers, they may be real rather than metaphorical, but that does not prevent them from carrying heavy symbolic baggage. The Israelites have been wandering around in the desert for quite a while. All kinds of exciting and terrifying things have happened to them, and given them proof, over and over again, that God goes with them to save them – in the first three verses of chapter 4 he has just helped them to victory over a formidable foe. But now the wanderers have hit a stagnant phase, where they just have to trudge along through the inhospitable terrain and they are, frankly, bored. They sound like spoiled children, cross and illogical: 'We're starving. There's no food, except the food we hate.'

At this point, we are told, God sends poisonous snakes to bite them – something with which many parents of spoiled toddlers at teatime may feel a sneaking sympathy. But the people have not wasted their years in captivity and their dark evenings round the camp fire in the wilderness. They know the creation stories, and they instantly recognize these snakes. The people recognize that they have given in to temptation, just as Adam and Eve did, and they quickly run to Moses to confess. And God gives Moses the strange remedy of a bronze snake to cure the fatal bite of the tempter.

How intriguing, then, Jesus's use of this bronze serpent is. John puts it in Jesus's conversation with Nicodemus, who is 'a teacher of Israel' yet does 'not understand these things'. Nicodemus should surely recognize Jesus as God's cure for the venom of the devil, but apparently he doesn't. Even the childish and grumbly children of Israel instantly spotted what God was up to, but not Nicodemus.

This whole conversation is about new life, being born again. The old life is the one that comes about through human sinfulness, and it leads inevitably to death. But the new life of the Spirit in Christ is the cure for everything associated with that ancient serpent in the garden, and it leads to life eternal. Jesus's death will be the cure for death, just as Moses's serpent was the cure for snake bites. Were there people in the company of the Israelites who were too stupid to run to the bronze serpent when they were bitten by a snake? Surely not. But there are those too blind to notice the healing sign lifted up in the cross.

Ephesians does not mention snakes, but it does further elucidate old lives and new. The old life led so inexorably to death that Ephesians just cuts out the middle bit, where you might temporarily believe yourself to be 'alive', and calls the whole thing 'death'. In that non-life it is as though we are all born with the fatal snake bite, and that's all there is to it. But God again provides the remedy, which is to cling to the cross of Christ and so to be raised from our death by Christ's death and resurrection. There is no medicine that we can manufacture to cure the old life. This passage is utterly emphatic about that. It cannot say often enough that this is entirely the work of God, his gift to us. And what he does is to give us a new life instead of the old one. We are created again, in Christ, and this time we will be able to do 'good works' (Ephesians 2.10), with no serpent to tempt us otherwise and fill us full of venom and death again.

But the problem with all of this talk of 'new life', wonderful though it is, is to find out what it means day to day. At the moment of conversion, and at moments of crisis or special meeting with God, you can feel an absolute clarity and certainty that this is, indeed, a new life, and that the old life has lost its hold upon you for ever, through the work of Christ. But in ordinary life, the old habits and failures and doubts reassert themselves time and time again, as if mocking any hope of real renewal. What Ephesians seems to be saying is that your situation is, as a matter of fact, now completely different, thanks to God, whether you always feel it or not. Wandering in the wilderness, the Israelites are no longer slaves, but they still grumble. Their status has changed, but their nature has to learn to respond. So with us. God has brought us into freedom and life – that is simply the case. The rest of our lives are about learning to live in our lively freedom.

The Fifth Sunday of Lent

—— ∿ ——

Jeremiah 31.31–34
Hebrews 5.5–10
John 12.20–33

At last a nice easy covenant. At last, Jeremiah seems to be suggesting, God will give up trying to teach us things and just zap us, changing us so that it becomes natural to us to know God. We won't need to be taught, we won't need to ask others, or experiment or learn about God through rehearsing past history. God will be part of us, written on our hearts. But I'm sorry to have to tell you that it isn't that simple. Although the emotion that is uppermost in this passage is longing – for the time when God and his people will be united – there is also anger and despair. The words that Jeremiah is speaking to his people on behalf of God are very hard to hear. For one thing, he is saying that the covenant that constituted them as God's people in the first place has been broken. The story of the Exodus is a foundational story for the people, and they base all their identity and their claims on God on that covenant. But Jeremiah says, very baldly, 'You broke that covenant. It's dead and gone.' He is also implying that the people are actually incapable of faithfulness and love of God. This new covenant, written on their hearts, may sound wonderful but it is actually a last resort. God has to do it this way because his people are incapable of keeping any other kind of covenant. Only by wiping the slate clean and starting again can God achieve what he set out to do when first he created people.

But if Jeremiah correctly describes failure and longing and hope, he does not yet know how God will fulfil this promise of a new covenant. Hebrews and John tell us the answer. The new covenant, carved on the human heart, is the promise God makes to us in Jesus. And suddenly the words 'written on the human heart' become not a comforting and painless metaphor but a terrible and searing reality. The cost of God keeping his promise to us, despite our inability to keep our side of it, is written on the human heart,

50

the human life and death of Jesus. The way God does what we cannot and will not do is to come himself as one of us, and keep both sides of the promise himself.

Hebrews and John both make clear that the undertone of anger and pain in Jeremiah's words of comfort is a proper echo. Hebrews's picture of Jesus crying and begging is hard for us to face, but it is the inevitable cost of the failure that Jeremiah highlights. Today's passage from John follows directly on from the triumphant entry into Jerusalem. Jesus's opponents are furious, and expect him to be more idolized and sought after than ever – and how right they are. The minute they've said it, in John 12.19, we're told in verse 20 that some Greeks come in search of Jesus. But at this moment, at the height of his fame and 'glory', Jesus starts to talk again about a different kind of glory altogether. The Greeks want to see Jesus, do they? Well, they and all the world will see him, lifted up in glory, all eyes upon him as he forces other rulers into submission. But the place of this triumph is the cross.

So when, in Jeremiah, God promises his people that they shall know him intimately, this is what he means. He is not talking about taking away our human nature and replacing it with something that will respond automatically to him, something that will recognize him not with love and fear and gratitude but as a computer recognizes a password. No, we will recognize him because he is one of us. We will see his struggle and his pain and his costly obedience and recognize it as the truth about our own humanity. Just as God promises in Jeremiah, Jesus is not our example – we are no more capable of copying him than Jeremiah's people were of keeping the covenant. In Jesus, God does both sides of the covenant – he makes the promise and faithfully keeps it on our behalf.

But if we begin to respond in awe to this new freedom, what might our response look like? Might it perhaps look a little like God's own response to our need? Sister Frances Dominica writes, 'If we really pray we take a big risk because by doing so we are saying, "Here I am, send me". God may take us at our word.'[1] If God's own way is one of costly involvement, perhaps we might need to risk that ourselves.

---

[1] Sister Frances Dominica in *Tradition and Unity*, ed. Dan Cohn-Sherbok, Bellew, 1991.

Palm Sunday

——— ∾ ———

Isaiah 50.4–9a
Philippians 2.5–11
Mark 14.1—15.47

It is as though there are any number of parallel stories in Mark's account of the trial and death of Jesus. The characters in each story are largely unaware of the others, though they may interact with each other to some extent. But each story believes it is the main story, carrying the meaning and purpose of the whole thing. The characters in each story seem to live in parallel time zones in which their decisions and actions make and remake history. They are the ones whose heroic lives and selfless decisions will be taught to generations of people to come as *the* history of the period, the only possible narrative. But the impact of Jesus's death is about to fuse all of these characters and these stories into something much bigger.

The first set of characters who believe themselves to be central are the people who oppose Jesus. The story they tell themselves is one in which they stand up for God against imposters and false prophets. Other people may be deceived by Jesus, but they are not. By their steadfastness and their willingness to take tough decisions they stand up for the purity of their religion and bring the people back to God. They know that their story is coming to a successful climax when the people they have been trying to lead towards God finally turn against Jesus and shout for his death. 'This is our story,' they say, 'the story of people who remained faithful to God.' But when their story merges into Jesus's, the faithfulness that they had so prided themselves on is judged to be utterly misguided.

Then there are the Roman authorities, represented by Pilate. The story Pilate tells himself is the one where he, a powerful and resourceful Roman governor, helps to uphold the Empire in this remote and troublesome spot. Pilate thinks this is the story of the Roman Empire, the most successful and civilized force ever. He knows that this incident in Palestine is a minor matter that will hardly be remembered in the history books at all, except as an example of his own strength and loyalty to the main story of the world. But when his narrative takes its place in Jesus's story, it turns out that he will chiefly be remembered as the man who put the hero to death.

What story does Judas tell himself, to justify his action and make himself believe that he is the one who truly knows where the plot is going? Is it a story in which he holds Jesus's fate and the fate of the other disciples in his hand? Is he convincing himself that he, Judas, is the one around whom all of this really revolves? The authorities need me, he tells himself. But he will not let himself see that they don't need him at all. They just want him to take the blame from them. They know perfectly well who Jesus is; they don't need Judas to show them. But they want to be able to say that Jesus was handed over to them, betrayed by his own followers. All through the last supper, Judas lives out his fantasy of himself in the centre, playing a clever double game as a secret agent. But in the end Judas sees where the real story was going, and sees his own shameful part in it.

Peter, too, gets a chance to see the real story and to put his own fantasy into its proper perspective. In his own story, Peter is Jesus's best friend, the one who has been with him at all the most exciting points of the ministry. He is the one who will finally persuade Jesus that his mission is really to throw out the Romans and proclaim the Kingdom of God. Jesus has some strange ideas at present about needing to die, but Peter is confident that he can talk him out of it. Talking has always been his strong point. But when he has talked himself into desertion and betrayal, that's when he gets a chance to be part of the main story, and even to take the plot on himself, after the resurrection, once he knows what the story is really about.

All of these stories suddenly coalesce and collide with reality around the cross of Christ. Suddenly it is clear that these are not short stories, with different possible endings, but one huge story, which is the story begun at the creation and not finished until Jesus returns to judge all the other stories about the world. This is the true story – the only true story – of God's faithful love for what he has made. All our stories are about how we journey into that one great story of creation and redemption.

Easter

Easter Day

——— ∾ ———

Isaiah 25.6–9
1 Corinthians 15.1–11
Mark 16.1–8

After all the horror, and the crowds and the noise of the day of Jesus's crucifixion, this chapter of Mark's Gospel starts quietly. We have already seen these women at the crucifixion scene, but we hardly noticed them there. Some of them were standing at 'a distance' (Mark 15.40–41), watching the terrible death of the man they had followed and supported. They made it their business to keep an eye on the body of Jesus, as it was taken down from the cross and laid – with kindness and courtesy, but without the reverence they knew it deserved – in the tomb. But although we are told their names, it is not until this final chapter that the women spring sharply into focus. Clearly, they had a strategy, unlike the male disciples. The disciples whose names we have heard all through the Gospel accounts of Jesus's ministry had a plan that led only to victory. The terrible end of all their hopes leaves them in disarray. They are notable by their absence in the whole of chapter 15 of Mark's account.

But the women have obviously got together and decided that, whatever happens, they will not lose sight of Jesus, and they will make it their business to treat him as their King, right up to the end. Perhaps things are easier for them because they are women. Perhaps their gender acts as a kind of cloak of anonymity to protect them from the kind of attack that Peter and the other disciples fear. Perhaps the very fact that they have decided what to do is giving them a kind of strength and fearlessness.

Their plan does have holes in it. They have bought all the spices they need to give the precious body its royal anointing. They could not have bought them on the Sabbath, surely? Does that mean that they, unlike the other disciples, had listened to Jesus and were actually expecting his death? Anyway, that part of the plan is in hand, and they know where they are going. But there is one big problem that they must have anticipated, which is the stone over the entrance to the tomb. In the original plan, had they expected at least one or two of the male disciples to be around to help? If so, it is now obvious either that the women have no idea where the men have run to, or that the men won't help. But the women are not going to let that stop them, although their whole plan stands or falls on being able to get to the body of Jesus. A kind of reckless determination has set in, and they will not acknowledge the possibility of failure. 'Someone will help us,' they tell each other. And if they think, 'But who will be around at this time in the morning, and who would be willing to help us anoint the body of a condemned criminal?' they don't say it out loud.

But then, as it happens, their plan, forged in fierce love, bravery and despair, hits a rather bigger plan. If the other disciples are thrown into terror and confusion by Jesus's death, these women are utterly confounded by his resurrection. The young man in white, who has so helpfully rolled the stone away, is saying things to them that they just cannot take in. They were not afraid of death, or of handling the dead body of the beloved master, but they are afraid of the empty tomb and the words of astonishing hope that are spoken to them. They had heard and understood Jesus talking about his own death, but apparently they had blocked out what he told them about the resurrection.

Why should hope and promise be harder to bear than death and despair? Why is it so hard to believe, now as then, that life and transformation and joy are as much part of the world and its maker as death and disintegration? The Christian hope of new life is not based on a kind of blind and meaningless optimism. On the contrary, all our hope is scarred with the wounds of the cross, and it is only hope because of that. It is the hope that God is indeed God. God is the creator, the source of all life, and nothing can make him not God. Our active, malignant sin that desires and makes death and destruction cannot force God into nothingness, and neither can our passive, despairing sin, that colludes with death and destruction because it can see no alternative.

So when the angel speaks the words of life and joy to us, let us believe them, and go and tell them, make them real and credible to others, show them the scars that are the source of life, not its end.

The Second Sunday of Easter

—— ～ ——

Acts 4.32–35
1 John 1.1—2.2
John 20.19–31

The recent popularity of *The Lord of the Rings* has helpfully given new vitality to the word 'fellowship'. The people who make up the 'fellowship of the ring' are not natural allies. They have little in common, and they join the fellowship with different personal priorities. But they are held together by the overriding need to save their countries from the menace of evil. They have to learn to trust one another, to rely on one another's skills and judgement, and allow for one another's particular weaknesses. This sense of struggle and adventure is a useful import into the rather debased Christian usage of 'fellowship', which is often used to mean little more than being temporarily nice to each other. We need to remember the sense of a continuing commitment and interdependence, and the reason why this fellowship is so vital. The world urgently needs it from us.

In the writings that we have under the name of 'John', 'fellowship' is rather more than an expedient device in the face of a particular threat. Entering into fellowship with each other is entering into the nature of God, and our failures in fellowship will obscure our witness to God. This is particularly striking in the talks that Jesus gives to his disciples at the Last Supper in John's Gospel (see, for example, John 17), but is very evident in the epistles of John too.

This opening section of 1 John echoes the beginning of the Gospel in its insistence that the witness to the particular life, death and resurrection of Jesus is a witness to the way the world is in its entirety. The life that pours out to those in fellowship with Jesus is the same vital source that gives life and breath and being to all that is. The world starts with the fellowship of God, Father, Son and Holy Spirit. Creation exists because God chose to share that fellowship.

This fellowship of ours, through which the world will begin to glimpse what God is like, can tolerate weakness and failure. The epistle is liberatingly clear that sin does not cease just because we have joined the fellowship of Jesus. What it cannot tolerate is lies. In the struggle to which we now commit ourselves, we have really to know our own and each other's strengths and weaknesses, and so the cause will be harmed if we are not truthful or if we lead ourselves or others to rely on us in areas where we cannot be reliable. It is, in any case, simply stupid to try to hide things from God, who is searing light, penetrating all darkness and deceit.

But both the Gospel and the epistle for today show God's enormous gentleness with us. God is not interested in guilt, but in a truthfulness that will build this vital fellowship. Isn't it moving that when Jesus comes to his frightened disciples, locked away in what they hope will be a safe house, he says not one word of condemnation to them? To these, his closest friends, who have betrayed and abandoned him to his horrible death, his first words are 'Peace be with you'. He must have said it with enormous conviction, because not one of the disciples tries to apologize or justify himself. They are all filled instantly with joy. That, they realize, is the only necessary response to the risen Christ. Even Thomas, the doubter who speaks for so many of us, is not greeted with any kind of impatience. Although there is certainly a teasing note in Jesus's voice as he speaks to Thomas, he knows what is needed to convince him, and he is happy to provide it.

The task that Jesus gives his disciples is an awesome one. He sends them out to build a fellowship that is strong through its truthfulness. They know that they lied about their own capabilities. They said they would never abandon Jesus, that they would follow him and stick with him through anything, and they know that their lies led to the disintegration of the fellowship at the cross of Christ. Now the new fellowship must be different. It must be based not on any foolish and unrealistic estimates of their own strength but on the vision of the searching and gentle God who has called them. It must give people a chance to glimpse what genuine fellowship, the life of Father, Son and Holy Spirit, might be like.

Very occasionally the Christian community can mirror that life, as in Acts 4, but more often it can only bear witness to the fact that the fellowship is made up of people who know their own weaknesses, and have needed and continue to need the forgiveness of God in Christ.

The Third Sunday of Easter

———— ∽ ————

Acts 3.12–19
1 John 3.1–7
Luke 24.36b–48

A puzzled seeker writes:

I've been interested in this Jesus movement for years, but I'm no closer to understanding it now that I'm an old man than I was all those years ago in Jerusalem. It started when my uncle took me on a business trip with him, to give me a chance to see the world, and to see if I'd like to go into the trade with him, since he'd got no sons of his own. Now I send my sons and grandsons, and just sit at home and reminisce. They tell me I've earned that right, after all these years, but I notice they don't listen to my stories!

Anyway, that first trip to Jerusalem, I was more interested to see the Temple than anything else. We weren't the most religious family in the world, but we knew that our people are special in God's eyes, and we did what we had to do to make sure God kept remembering that. So I pestered my uncle, and that's how we happened to be in the Temple the afternoon a lame man got healed. My uncle insisted it was a fraud, but he didn't see the expression on the man's face. He was shocked, more than any-thing. Of course, everyone came running, hoping for a show, but the two men who'd healed him acted as though it was the kind of thing that happened every day. They said that if we believed in Jesus, our sins would be forgiven and we'd be able to do things like that too.

My uncle didn't want to hang around, wasting valuable trad-ing time, but he let me go out in the evenings and sniff around. I found out quite a lot more about these Jesus people. Their Jesus had been killed by the Romans, though they seemed to blame us for it, saying that if our people had read the scriptures properly, we'd know that Jesus was the Messiah. They were causing quite a stir in the city, with their preaching and healing, and they'd made quite a lot of converts. I liked them. They seemed kind, and they talked a lot about God loving us and forgiving us, if we believed in Jesus. I thought it would be good to be forgiven. Us traders are always breaking the Law, in little ways. You can't get a boat to stop on the Sabbath, and you can't be too choosy about what you eat when you're sealing a deal. So we've got no hope of being righteous that way.

Even after we went home, I never entirely forgot about the Jesus people, and it wasn't long before they'd spread to my part of the world. So obviously I wasn't the only one who thought they were making a kind of sense. I used to sneak out to their meetings sometimes and try to find out more. The main thing they were saying was that you can only find out about God through this Jesus. They said that Jesus showed us what God is like, and that Jesus came to die to take away our sins, and that he rose from the dead and is alive now. Apparently, some of the people had met people who'd met Jesus after he rose again, so they knew it was true.

That was all very interesting, but that main question kept niggling at me. What do I have to do to know that I'm right with God? Now that I'm old and I know I can't live for ever, it's become the most important question in my life. I haven't been a bad person, but I haven't been a good one either. Is it enough just to believe in Jesus? Some of these Christians seem to say that's all there is. But some of them say that if you do believe, it will change the way you live, and you will be good and loving. If so, I can't say that I've seen any proof of it. These Christians are as good at hating each other as anyone else. There are at least two different lots of them just in my town, not speaking to each other. How can I believe what they say about us being the children of God, free and forgiven, if they can't even forgive each other? They're good at blaming others, like my people, or the Romans, or some other leader who doesn't say things their way. Perhaps they should try blaming themselves for a change. If they were to say, 'We crucified Jesus, and we keep doing it, but he still forgives us and trusts us,' then I might be able to believe that he'll forgive me too.

The Fourth Sunday of Easter

— ∾ —

Acts 4.5–12
1 John 3.16–24
John 10.11–18

Today's readings are deeply challenging. Christian mission has sometimes been done as though determined to prove that we are right and everyone else is wrong, whereas all of today's writers think that Christians must preach and show Jesus Christ because that is actually how the world is.

In Acts, Peter and John have been arrested. They healed a lame man and then preached to the astonished crowds that gathered. But whatever the ostensible reason for the arrest, the question that the religious authorities ask is a telling one. 'How did you do it, and whose side are you on?' is what it boils down to. The Temple committee are already a bit suspicious of this new movement but, on the other hand, the healing did take place in the Temple, so it's possible that they are hoping to make religious capital out of it for themselves. If Peter and John are amenable, and say that they work through the power and in the name of God, then perhaps a happy compromise for all can be reached.

But Peter and John are not in the business of compromise. They are filled with the courage of the Holy Spirit, the life-giver, and they answer the question with alarming forthrightness. There is only one name, Peter says, that connects heaven and earth, that expresses the way in which God relates to us, and that assures us of God's powerful and saving love for us: Jesus.

Peter's certainty may sound embarrassingly harsh. Interestingly, several of the commentaries I checked chose not to say anything at all about this verse. The claims that Christians make on behalf of Christ just are demanding and exclusive of other descriptions of the world, and there is no getting away from that. But if you look at them in the light of today's other two readings, the strong impression emerges that Christians can only make these claims about Christ by living them.

In the Gospel reading, Jesus describes his ministry as that of the shepherd. This metaphor is one that has inspired countless sermons and pictures, but I haven't seen one where the frightened sheep have our human faces, watching our shepherd, Jesus, fighting off a pack of wolves. Our instinct is to run, scatter, and thereby make ourselves easier targets for being picked off by the wolves. The shepherd is fighting, desperately, to keep us together, to keep the whole flock safe. It is only our trust in him that enables us to stay there, shivering but together. Even so, every so often one of us makes a panicky break for it, but then the well-loved voice of the shepherd calls that one by name and brings it back to its senses.

Love, cost and purpose are the themes of the description that Jesus highlights, but purpose is the one that often gets left out. One flock, one shepherd, Jesus says, that's the goal. The flock will come really to know the voice of Jesus, and the love of Jesus, which is also the voice and the love of God.

The sheep come to know the voice of the shepherd because it is the voice that they have learned to associate with care, safety, warmth, food. In a crisis they will trust the shepherd because he has proved himself trustworthy before, in providing for their basic needs. The sheep would not have come to trust the shepherd if he had come out and given them a sermon a day. His voice would not be the one they loved and believed if they had not experienced it first as the voice of practical care.

This is certainly the point being made in 1 John. 'Let us love not in word or speech but in truth and action,' the epistle urges. The words are the easy bit. They cost the speaker very little, but equally they yield very little. The sheep wander off, unfed and unprotected, because they do not recognize this unfamiliar voice. It has never done anything for them. Christian shepherds, like Jesus, have to build up the trust of the sheep, and be prepared to redeem it at great personal cost, if necessary. We have to live in the world as though we really did believe that Jesus, the good shepherd who lays down his life to save us, is the way of God. We have to live together, one flock with one shepherd, as though we knew that this is what we were made for. Any other way of living is out of tune with the whole purpose of the universe. Luckily, the voice of the good shepherd is still heard in the Holy Spirit, since we still need to learn how to be shepherds ourselves.

The Fifth Sunday of Easter

——— ∽ ———

Acts 8.26–40
1 John 4.7–21
John 15.1–8

The writings of John, both in the Gospel and the epistles, are baf-flingly determined not to come down on one side or the other of the 'chicken or egg' question. Which comes first, love of God or love of our neighbour? Which is more important, being or doing? Are we saved by grace or by works? Instinctively, temperamentally, most people come down on one side or another, and hear only those parts of the good news of Jesus Christ that seem to reinforce what is natural to us. Some people instinctively hear the message con-tained in Jesus's first public statement in Luke's Gospel: 'good news to the poor, release to the captives, sight to the blind, freedom for the oppressed' (Luke 4.18–19). Surely this is the heart of Jesus's message, they argue, and Christian witness to Christ is most faithful when it is actively doing things to improve life for society. Other people instinctively see that all of Jesus's activity arises out of his times of silence and prayer. His ministry starts not as he stands up and speaks, but as he wrestles alone in the desert.

The problem is that today's Gospel and epistle, like most of the New Testament, do not let you see that as an either/or. Instead, they argue, it is always both. Both epistle and Gospel are talking about the nature of God, which we contemplate with awe, but which we are also drawn into. 1 John talks about love as the funda-mental nature and sign of God. Where you see love, you know the presence of God. Out of love, God the Son comes to die, so that we can be drawn back into the love of Father, Son and Holy Spirit. In God, then, love is not an abstract quality, but one that we experi-ence very directly as *activity*. God *acts* lovingly towards us, and that is how we know that he is indeed love. In God, being and doing are not separate – he is love and acts lovingly. For us, that is not always the case because, unlike God, we are not yet complete.

The people to whom 1 John is addressed are presumably people who have accepted the saving love of God with gratitude, but who are still able to act without love to one another because in them, as in us, love has a beginning and a finite end. The great aim of our life is to make the beginning and the end of love get further and further apart in us, so that there is more and more room, more and more things we can love. In God love has no beginning and no end. As the great seventeenth-century poet John Donne said in one of his Christmas sermons, God's love is like a circle – endless.

The Gospel is talking about another one of God's inalienable characteristics, which is life. 1 John's language about love can sound a bit repetitive and soft-edged, despite the urgency of what is being said, but if you put it alongside today's Gospel, the reason for the urgency becomes clearer. God is the only source of life. If you pick flowers, they die. If you take people away from God, they die. It is not that this is a punishment, exactly; it is more that it is just a fact of life. So only branches grafted into the true vine can live and bear fruit. That is why this choice between being and doing is a false one. You are either alive with the life of God, the life in which there is no distinction between what God is and what he does, or you are not alive at all.

Many of us would quite like to rely on the life-giving love of God for ourselves without having to change too much. Philip, in today's story from Acts, wouldn't understand the question 'Should I spend time in prayer or should I go out and preach?' He has allowed himself to be very directly grafted into the life of God, so that everyone he meets is an opportunity waiting to be shown the love of God. An Ethiopian eunuch, miles from home, reading the Bible? When did you last expect to find someone like that waiting for you? Most of us wouldn't know such an opportunity if it passed us by, not even in a golden carriage full of treasure, and so we miss the chance that Philip seized to work with God. And on his way home, 'as he happened to be passing through the region' of Azotus, he preached there too. 'What, travel through a whole region without showing people the love of God?' Philip asks. 'Are you mad?'

The Sixth Sunday of Easter

—— ⚋ ——

Acts 10.44–48
1 John 5.1–6
John 15.9–17

The desire for certainty goes very deep, and all of today's readings look at that longing with sympathy, though the answers they give are as challenging as they are reassuring.

In the Gospel, Jesus is at last giving his disciples 'commandments'. If the disciples have been listening to Jesus throughout the weeks and months before this, they must have some inkling already about how Jesus interprets God's commandments to his people. Underlying the great commandments given by God to Moses is the imperative that his people should show by their lives what their God is like. This commandment Jesus has fulfilled utterly. Through all his life he has kept the commandment to love God, be loved by God and to show God's love, and that is the commandment that he now passes on to his disciples.

If the commandments given to Moses have proved difficult to interpret and fulfil, then Jesus's retelling of them has proved even harder. How do we know if we have fulfilled this great command to love one another? The example that Jesus gives, of his own willingness to die for his friends, is not a comforting one. Is that, then, to be the measure of love? Well, the Gospel suggests, it may need to be sometimes. But the verses that directly follow the giving of this commandment suggest that there are other interim measures too. One is the insistent changing of roles that is so characteristic of Jesus's teaching. 'I have called you friends', he says, 'because I have made known to you everything that I heard from my Father.' The sharing that characterizes Father and Son is extended to us. We are not simply issued with instructions that we must follow without needing to understand them. Instead we are invited to God's table, to eat and discuss and share in his great plan for the world. So one mark of our 'love' for one another and God will presumably be our willingness to extend this invitation to others. 'Come and join us at

God's table, come and help us to work out with God what to do next.' If God makes friends, not servants, so should Christians.

The second measure of our success at 'loving' that these verses suggest is 'bearing fruit'. Bringing others to share in the life and love of God will make us more loving. Anyone who has had any experience in Christian evangelism, whether in word or deed or both, would I think agree with that. It is deeply challenging and enlarging to see the word of God at work in the lives of others, and to see that before you and your feeble attempt at love got anywhere near the situation, God's love was already at work.

That is certainly the experience of Peter and his hearers as they watch Cornelius and his household respond to the love of God. They hear these strangers praising God long before they have gone through all the proper forms, and they realize that their own love for the Gentiles has been much smaller than God's. If they were looking for certainty about the next step in relation to the Gentiles, then they are given it abundantly. They see the Holy Spirit poured out with unmistakable power – and notice that that power is proved not just by the use of tongues, but by the praise of God. Of course, the certainty experienced by these witnesses is not easily transmitted to those who weren't present, as you will discover if you read the next chapter of Acts or Paul's letter to the Galatians.

1 John combines both love and the Holy Spirit in its explanation of Christian certainty. Like the Gospel, 1 John suggests that the commandment we are given – the thing we have to do to know that we are in the right – is to love God and love each other. Like Acts, it suggests that it is the Holy Spirit rather than our own innate discernment that leads us to spot the love of God at work. 1 John also reintroduces the sombre note of suffering sounded by the Gospel. The cross of Christ is not a past thing that has been superseded by the praise, joy and certainty of the Spirit. The Spirit witnesses constantly to the truth of the life, death and resurrection of Jesus which, in its totality, is the way of God's victory in the world.

Today's readings imply that certainty comes through sharing our faith, praising God and loving one another. Each one of those activities makes the others more and more possible and natural, and brings us closer and closer to the life of God, Father, Son and Holy Spirit.

The Seventh Sunday of Easter

―― ∼ ――

Acts 1.15–17, 21–26
1 John 5.9–13
John 17.6–19

What would you like people to pray for on your behalf? What is your most usual – truthful – prayer request? Does Jesus's prayer for his disciples match your expectations in any way?

This prayer comes as Jesus prepares to leave his disciples and, although the context here is the preparation for the crucifixion, it is a good prayer to think about in connection with the ascension as well. At the heart of it is Jesus's love for the disciples, but also his certainty that the Father, too, loves these people who have recognized and cared for the Son. More than that, even, Jesus's prayer reveals to the disciples that God the Father actually gave them to the Son, to be his companions and witnesses. They may have thought that they chose Jesus or, if they were feeling very humble, that Jesus chose them, but now they discover that God himself chose them for Jesus because he loved them. This prayer is in the nature of an account-giving, as Jesus explains to the Father what he has done with the people the Father entrusted to him.

But now that that phase of Jesus's ministry is past, Jesus moves on to direct prayer for these people he has come to love. What does he pray for? Well, he does pray for protection, which must be high on most people's wish list, but perhaps not all of us wish to be protected so that we may be one (v. 11). Yet this is the central force of this extraordinary prayer, and it reveals something of the purpose of Jesus's own ministry. All those who accept Jesus know that they are in the active, dynamic presence of the will of God. Where Jesus is, there God's purpose is being fulfilled. This is the quality that Jesus now thanks his Father for in the disciples. They have believed that fundamental fact about Jesus – that he was sent by the Father – and so they have been able to share in the unity between Father and Son. As they proclaim the presence of God in Jesus, they themselves step into that place, or that way of being, where God's will is done. This is to be their 'joy' (v. 13), as it has been Jesus's joy, to do the will of the Father, and so to be part of the spread of the Kingdom of God.

So Jesus prays for his disciples that they will be protected from the 'evil one', whose purpose, it seems, is to destroy Christian unity and so destroy Christian witness to the unity of Father and Son. And he prays that they may have joy. Unfortunately, just as the description of protection may not be the most common one, nor is the description of joy. Christian 'joy' involves being hated and rejected by a world that does not recognize the unity of Father and Son. It involves witnessing to the truth of the incarnation by holding on to each other under all circumstances, and never allowing the world's scepticism or hostility to divide us, just as it did not divide Father and Son in Jesus's earthly ministry.

This prayer of Jesus's is a very revealing bit of doctrinal theology, and it intimately connects the being of God and the being of the Church. It is at the heart of the Christian proclamation of God that the Father is most fully revealed in the Son and the Son in the Spirit. Trinitarian theology insists that 'unity' is an active concept, shown forth in dynamic interdependence and self-giving. It would hardly need to be called 'unity' at all if God were one in a simple and undifferentiated way.

So we are used to the idea that implicit in the whole of Jesus's earthly ministry is the unity of Father and Son. Everything Jesus does and is, he does and is in obedience to the Father and to demonstrate and exercise the will of the Father. But we may not be so used to the next step that the author of St John's Gospel takes in today's readings. Jesus comes to bring the active, redeeming presence of God into our human situation. We are called to bear witness to that. Jesus does this because he is one with the Father. We can only do our witnessing job if we are one with Jesus. We cannot be one with Jesus while clearly at odds with each other. How can witnesses who squabble about the truth possibly bear witness to the unity of Father, Son and Spirit?

As Jesus ascends to the Father, the Christian community is given the particular responsibility of witnessing to what we have learned about the unity of Father, Son and Holy Spirit.

Day of Pentecost

———— ∽ ————

Acts 2.1–21
Romans 8.22–27
John 15.26–27; 16.4b–15

The Holy Spirit has been in danger in recent years of becoming the soppy one of the Trinity. Think about it for a bit – the Holy Spirit doesn't go off and do uncomfortable and challenging things like getting crucified. The Holy Spirit gives spectacular gifts that add a distinct touch of excitement to what could otherwise become rather dreary religious lives. The Holy Spirit can be described as the 'comforter', which sounds just lovely. The Holy Spirit is very politically correct and not at all gender-specific. The Holy Spirit likes to leave things to the last minute, like us, and works best if you stand up unprepared and allow the Spirit to take over. S/he really hates to be called upon by untrusting people who fussily want to prepare several days in advance. All in all, the Holy Spirit is the acceptable face of the Trinity.

Unfortunately, this picture of the Holy Spirit bears no resemblance at all to the Holy Spirit as depicted in the New Testament. Today's reading from Acts does sound, initially, rather exciting. We might feel, a shade wistfully, that if we had had tongues of fire resting on our heads then we might be able to match the sudden boldness of the disciples as they stand up and witness to Jesus. But when Peter begins to talk, fuelled by the power of the Holy Spirit, what he is led to talk about is judgement. The coming of the Holy Spirit emphasizes the finality and totality of what God has done in Jesus Christ. The way in which people react to Jesus seals their fate just as surely as if the world had indeed come to an end with 'portents in the heaven above and signs on the earth below' (v. 19). And if Peter's words today ring with excitement and conviction, he is to spend the rest of his days witnessing to this truth he once denied, and he is to pay for it with his life.

The Gospel reading also talks about the Holy Spirit in terms of judgement. With exactly the same theological force as in Acts, John

70

says that the work of the Holy Spirit is to point out the consequences of how we respond to Jesus. The Holy Spirit comes to
prove conclusively that the world has got most of its judgements
skewed. The world judged Jesus to be mad and dangerous, and it
condemned him to death, thereby proving that it didn't know right
from wrong. The Holy Spirit comes to reverse that judgement, and
turn the tables. Those who convicted Jesus of sin are now shown to
be the deluded sinners. The Holy Spirit comes to prove that Jesus is
the one who knows the truth, and that is because Jesus's judgements are the same as God's. The Spirit of truth comes to bear
witness to the unity of Father and Son and to empower us to do the
same.

Romans 8 speaks quite graphically of the work of the Spirit in
terms of childbirth. Not the happy, sanitized version, where the
cleaned-up baby smiles up at its well-rested parents, but the real
version where there is far too much groaning and pain and blood.
This is a good metaphor, Paul suggests, because the point of all that
anguish is the child that is to be born. In the middle of labour it is
possible almost to forget that it will ever end and that there will be
an outcome. But the Holy Spirit, like the midwife, keeps the world
straining and pushing. 'Come on, you're nearly there, I can see the
head now,' the Holy Spirit shouts, reminding us constantly why we
are doing this.

The Holy Spirit knows how to interpret the anguish of the world.
The Holy Spirit has seen the image of Jesus forming more and more
clearly in so many people that, in the midst of our cries we can hear
the words, 'It's all right. This is how it is supposed to be. Nothing
has gone wrong. Keep hoping, keep working. The end is in sight.'
Hope is one of the hallmarks of the Holy Spirit, according to
Romans 8, and this is no mindless self-deceiving hope but the truthful hope of one who knows the will of God.

All of these readings suggest that the work of the Holy Spirit is to
bear witness to the truth of Jesus Christ, and to enable our witness
to that same truth. Sometimes that will be accompanied by gratify-
ing gifts of power and sometimes it will involve a complete surren-
der of human power, to the point of death. But wherever the Holy
Spirit witnesses, there is judgement. 'Do you choose for or against
God?' the Holy Spirit asks, echoing the life and work of Jesus.

Ordinary Time

Trinity Sunday

───── ∾ ─────

Isaiah 6.1–8
Romans 8.12–17
John 3.1–17

John Donne, the great seventeenth-century Anglican poet, said in his *Litanie* that the doctrine of the Trinity is 'Bones to Philosophy, but milk to faith'.[1] Bones and milk are both provided by today's readings.

The belief that God is Trinity is the foundation for the belief that God is also love. If God were not Trinity, the most we could say with absolute confidence would be that God occasionally – or even regularly – chooses to act lovingly, but not that he is, in himself, love. Belief in God the Trinity says that before there was anything external to God towards which God could act lovingly, God's being was still expressed in the love between Father, Son and Spirit. This 'love' of God is not an abstract quality, unrecognizable by the usual marks of what we humans would call love. It is personal, dynamic and creative. It is full of delight and generosity. It longs for the rest of the world to see the loveliness of the beloved. We, God's creation, come to be out of the exuberance and sheer vitality of that love, and we are designed to share in it, to be drawn more and more into the reality of the loving God.

That is why verse 16 is the climax of the odd, teasing conversation between Jesus and Nicodemus. 'This is the point of it all,' Jesus says, 'that God's beloved people may live with us for ever.'

Does Nicodemus understand that? It is very hard to tell, just as it is hard to tell what he is doing there at all, creeping about in the dead of night like a young revolutionary rather than a weighty religious leader of a people who have made a sensible compromise with their irreligious rulers.

───────────

[1] John Donne, 'A litanie' in *John Donne: Selections from Divine Poems, Sermons, Devotions, and Prayers*, ed. John Booty, The Classics of Western Spirituality, Paulist Press, 1990, p. 87.

From his opening words, Jesus wrong-foots Nicodemus. Nicodemus has rehearsed what he is going to say to open the conversation. He pays tribute to Jesus's ministry, while at the same time making understated claims for his own credentials. 'I'm someone who can recognize the activity of God,' he says in effect, 'and you're really doing very well, old chap.' To which Jesus answers, in effect, 'How would you know?' All through the sharp-edged conversation, Nicodemus is trying to get things back on track, back into normal conversational and debating mode, and Jesus won't let him. The activity of God cannot be ordered by your little checklists, he says to Nicodemus. You have to tear them up and be prepared to start again.

Nicodemus, like all religious people throughout the ages, believes to some extent that God is love. But he believes that God's love is measured and sensible, and follows a set of rules. He believes that Jesus's healings are, largely, consonant with the activity of God, but he has some worries about them, which is presumably why he is here, to get Jesus to fill in the proper forms. And he does deserve some credit for this – many of his colleagues couldn't or wouldn't see even this far into the love of God. But it is not far enough, because all Jesus's replies to Nicodemus suggest that Nicodemus has to let go of all the measures that he has been using, and launch out into the unfathomable reality of the totality of God's love. God does not love when we have met the requirements, or when we have changed enough to be lovable, or when we were lucky enough to be born in one race or sex. God just loves. And trying to measure the love of God is like trying to control the wind. God will do anything for this world he loves, including coming himself, the Son, to die for it. To understand this is to be, in Jesus's words, born again, to start the world again, learning to walk and speak and think and grow in a world where the love of God is the breath that we breathe, so that our every response to the world around is informed by that love.

So don't try to measure the wind of God's love, Paul argues, just go with it, let it breathe through you and power you – God's Spirit, a totally renewable power source. To be filled with the vitality of God's love is to share in God's relationship with God and to know ourselves beloved. It is also to share in God's wild love for the world. Send us! we exclaim with Isaiah. Paul and John both warn us that our love must be as insane as God's. No reintroducing the checklists, no loving on our terms only. God the Son preferred to go to the cross rather than force his creation into a dutiful, fearful obedience to the Father, so that must be our choice also, if necessary.

Proper 4

———— ∾ ————

Deuteronomy 5.12–15
2 Corinthians 4.5–12
Mark 2.23—3.6

Today's passages send out an alarmingly confusing set of messages. On the one hand, Deuteronomy tells us how vital it is to keep the Sabbath, while Jesus seems to suggest that we can sit a bit more lightly to that in certain circumstances. The Pharisees are obeying the scriptures and Jesus, apparently, is not. Next confusion: Jesus is acting with authority and power, and that makes his message incredible to those around him, while Paul is weak and vulnerable and that seems to prove to the Corinthians that he can't really be God's messenger.

So let's start with the confusion over the Sabbath, since that is probably slightly more easily resolved. Jesus's words cannot be taken as validating the state of affairs that we have now reached in Britain, where there is no recognizable, shared culture of rest and relaxation, no protected time for families to spend together, no obvious evening where people sit down and talk to each other and remind themselves of what is really important in life. Sharing Friday evening Sabbath meals with Jewish friends has been a revelation to me of what we have lightly lost. In eating, talking, remembering and sharing, all in the context of prayer, it is not just a family that is being built up, but also a whole society. This is where we might remember what we value, what we were made for.

So when Jesus picks food and heals the sick on the Sabbath, he is not saying, I think, that it's OK to go to Tesco seven days a week, but reminding his listeners of what the Sabbath does. The Sabbath recreates us as more than just people who live to work. It recreates us as images of God. There is no record of Jesus being criticized for doing trivial and irrelevant things on the Sabbath, things that could easily be done any other time. Instead, he is being criticized by those who have forgotten the real meaning of the Sabbath, and its witness to the creative God, who delights in what he has made and wants that delight to have time to flourish in others. If the hungry and the sick are to be able to share God's joy, they need to be fed or healed. But the bored and the overworked and overfed need to rediscover the Sabbath.

What makes Jesus's use of his authority so unacceptable to his listeners in this context is that he is reasserting the claim of God on their lives, whereas they had been assuming that the commandments are there so that we can assert our rights over God. 'See, God,' we say, 'we have kept our part, now behave properly towards us.' While Jesus is saying, 'Come and live in God's world and his life, come and be recreated in his image and delight in his world.'

In all of what he does, Jesus offers two pictures of life, only one of which is real. We either live with God's life or we don't actually live at all. And that is exactly what Paul is saying. The creative power of the God who said 'Let there be light' is alive through Christ, and we are privileged to share in it. This is not a power that is innate to us. By ourselves, we are 'clay jars', just as, by himself, Adam was a clay figure until God breathed life into him. The life is God's, not ours. That means that a lot of the self-perpetuating myth of life with which we live for most of the time has to be relinquished. This myth says that being properly alive means being well, rich, happy and – preferably – sexually fulfilled. It is a myth that says that immediate gratification is the goal of human life. But Paul argues that real life, the life that flows from God, returns to God, and that knows how to live in the world that God has made, looks like Jesus. We have no other model of a human being fully alive, only Jesus. And that makes authentic Christian life a little harder to spot. It might not always be as tough as Paul's life was, but it can't automatically be measured by other definitions of 'success'. Jesus's brief life ends in a horrible death and a failure, apparently, to impose his understanding of God on even his closest followers. And yet Jesus was so fully alive and vital with God's own life that even death could not extinguish him, but is forced to serve God's resurrection life, and become the source of life for the world. Paul's life is a true response to the boundless life of Jesus because, like Jesus's life, it brings others into the life of God. It is life because it is lifegiving for others.

Proper 5

———— ❧ ————

Genesis 3.8–15
2 Corinthians 4.13—5.1
Mark 3.20–35

Things are moving at a relentless pace for Jesus in these early chapters of Mark's Gospel. Already he is being followed everywhere he goes by large crowds of people. Already he has made bitter enemies out of the local clergy. Some of the people who follow him are just hoping to be in on the action, and they don't much care if it is a healing or a pitched battle that they witness. But some of the crowd can already be called 'disciples' (see Mark 3.7), and they would no doubt believe that they are following Jesus out of conviction. From them, Jesus has just chosen the twelve, who are to be particularly closely identified with his mission throughout their lives.

And now he goes home, Mark tells us, and even here the crowd press around him so thickly that his family begin to get rather peeved. His antics are annoying the neighbours and getting the family a bad reputation. Perhaps they had thought that Jesus's healing and teaching was like a job – he could go out to do it by day and come back to a normal family life in the evenings. This great heaving, struggling mass of people, with their noise and their litter and their complete lack of concern for any other part of Jesus's life is not at all what they expected. They begin to be rather afraid that the experts from Jerusalem are right, and Jesus has gone mad. After all, no one in their right mind would want to be the centre of such scenes, would they?

But if the anger and bewilderment of Jesus's family is comprehensible, the scribes are up to something a bit more sinister. Jesus's family are reacting much as any other family might whose brother or son has catapulted to superstardom overnight. They knew he was something special, but they hadn't anticipated it having this kind of effect on all their lives. But the scribes are not bewildered and overwhelmed – they are appalled. They cannot allow all this huge crowd of people to believe in Jesus, and perhaps even pass on their belief to yet more people, because Jesus is not singing from their hymn sheet. He has already made it perfectly clear that he will not dutifully follow the rules, and the scribes are afraid of losing control of large proportions of the population. Perhaps they are not just cynically thinking of their own prestige and pockets. Perhaps they are genuinely devout students of scripture, and are shocked at what they have heard about Jesus forgiving sins and healing on the Sabbath. He is not obeying the clear word of scripture, so he must be wrong, whatever the crowds think, and however commendable his healings appear to be. They see his power and they know only two sources of such power – God or the devil. It can't come from God, because God can only work according to the scripture, so it must come from the devil.

Jesus's answer asks them to look not just at the theory of God, but also at the reality. The simple fact of the matter is that everything Jesus has done is good. It has resulted in the restoration of the children of God to the human community. Everywhere he goes, madness, evil and sickness are banished. The voices of the demon-possessed call out to Jesus throughout these first chapters of Mark, and they call out in fear, in longing, and in recognition of the power of God, so alien to the small, mad, dark power that tries to control them but is nowhere near strong enough to blind them to the reality of God. In St Luke's Gospel, Jesus begins his public ministry by saying in scriptural words what we are about to see: good news is brought to the poor, the captives are released, the blind see and the oppressed go free (Luke 4.18). But here in Mark's Gospel, Jesus simply does God's word; he performs it in action, rather than proclaiming it in words. Those who read God's word should surely recognize it in action. Evil does not work against itself, Jesus says. Recognize the strong, liberating might of God, come to put an end to all captivity. Do not dare to confuse the action of God to free his people with the action of the enslaving enemy.

This, Jesus says, is the 'blasphemy against the Holy Spirit'. It is the willingness to confuse God's living, liberating Spirit with the death-dealing, imprisoning spirit of evil. You cannot confuse them by accident. You can only do it if you wilfully reject God, and prefer to be bound yourself and see others in chains than accept God's redemption in Christ.

Proper 6

—— ∾ ——

Ezekiel 17.22–24
2 Corinthians 5.6–17
Mark 4.26–34

Paul's argument in this section of 2 Corinthians is complex and far-reaching. He is putting forward a whole new theory of reality and knowledge. Christians, he argues, carry their own reality system around with them, and they have to learn how to make judgements based on that reality and not be fooled by the virtual reality that other people still live in. There will sometimes be some very uncomfortable dissonance between the two 'realities', which can confuse and alarm Christians, and Paul is trying to give the Corinthian church some pointers, to help them to judge wisely.

One of the things that makes negotiating this new Christian world particularly difficult is that our bodies are obstinately stuck in the old reality. They will insist on seeing the world with old eyes, and on wanting the kind of comfort and security that they were always used to seeking. Interestingly, Paul does not say that our bodily needs are wicked. There is no simplistic dualism between body and spirit, wrong and right. Instead, he just says, 'Don't worry'. What we increasingly have to learn is that these old bodies are not our home. Although we are not urged to try to shed them too quickly, we still have to learn not to trust their judgements about the world.

So, for example, we have to learn not simply to trust what we see. Our old way of seeing things may suggest that we are walking into danger or, at the very least, discomfort, and try to stop us. But we have to remember that we are now walking with a different map. 'We walk by faith, not by sight,' Paul says (2 Corinthians 5.7). It is not any longer our main aim to please ourselves and keep ourselves safe. Now we are working to please God.

That is going to affect the way we judge other people too. It sounds, from verses 11–13, as though the Corinthian church has been judging Paul by other kinds of standards and finding him wanting. There seems to be a suggestion that they would like Paul to stop giving them sensible instructions and telling them off. Other religious leaders, they say, fall into ecstatic fits, and lead worshippers into exciting frenzies of adoration. You just keep writing us letters, they complain. I could concentrate on charismatic devotions, Paul says, but it wouldn't do you any good. My worship of God is between God and me, but my job in relation to you is to teach you about the love of God in Christ, and to teach you how to see the world in the light of that reality.

Paul knows that what he is describing is difficult. He himself has had to learn how to judge differently and by completely different criteria. After all, he made his own independent judgement about Jesus, and it led him to persecute Christians. He used all his old standards of knowledge and judgement, and decided that Jesus and his followers were enemies of God. His conversion turned all his own knowledge and understanding completely on its head.

Paul had obviously believed that his primary religious role, in the old days, was to keep people out, by force if necessary. If they did not agree with him then they had to go. Now, through the eyes of Christ, he sees the world very differently. Now he sees that God in Christ seeks to bring people in, not keep them out, and so those of us who try to walk by faith, not sight, have to do the same. Every single Christian is given the opportunity to become part of God's reconciling work in Christ. We can become his ambassadors, Paul says (v. 20). Where we are is God's country, God's reality, where the main currency is forgiveness. It is not our job any longer to make judgements according to any other criteria. All the criteria that Paul had available to him previously led him to believe that Jesus, who died a criminal's death on the cross, was a sinner, and just look how wrong he was. All we can do now is affirm, loudly and constantly, that if we walk in Jesus's reality, then we are forgiven and brought into God's home.

To change our standards of judgement so completely is very hard. But we make it, perhaps, even more difficult than we need to by assuming that what is called for is something huge. It needn't be, Jesus suggests. It might be just getting up day by day and doing what has to be done. Walking by faith, as Paul calls it, might just be a matter of putting one foot in front of the other, and moving imperceptibly into God's reality.

Proper 7

—— ∽ ——

Job 38.1–11
2 Corinthians 6.1–13
Mark 4.35–41

In today's readings we have two different, and potentially incompatible, views of how God works.

The reading from Job and the reading from the Gospel seem to have one vision, which is of the colossal and unquestionable power of God. In Job, God finally rounds on Job's so-called friends, with their endless quasi-theological advice about what has caused Job's sufferings. At last, God speaks for himself. He does not deign to explain himself, since it is clear that his hearers are too stupid to understand, even if it was God's concern to make himself comprehensible. Instead, God sets about pointing out exactly why Job, his friends – and we – are unfit to question the Lord. 'What exactly *do* you understand?' God asks, and the implication is obviously 'nothing'. Nothing about how the world functions is either understood or controlled by us, and yet we are indignant that God does not lay his plans before us. We are like tone-deaf concert-goers sitting and grumpily complaining that we don't understand this thing called 'music'.

As Jesus stills the storm in today's Gospel reading we see again the awesome power of God. The unpredictable and merciless forces of nature suddenly respond like obedient children to the voice of Jesus, and the disciples are amazed. They were already terrified by the storm, but they are almost equally terrified by its sudden cessation at Jesus's command. When Jesus asks them, 'Why are you afraid, have you no faith?' the Gospel is deliberately unclear about which fear he means.

These statements of the inexorable power of God need to be heard, perhaps today more than ever, when a debilitating theology of the 'niceness' of God can all too easily portray him as utterly ineffectual. But we have to be careful to allow God to define power, and not to impose our own longed-for definitions on him. Otherwise what Paul is saying in 2 Corinthians looks simply contradictory. Paul is talking about the power of God at work in his ministers as they suffer 'beatings, imprisonments, riots' and all manner of other sufferings (2 Corinthians 6.5). And the Jesus who commands the storm is soon to be forced on to the cross. So what is God's power like?

The strange thing about God's response to Job and his friends is that it is almost exactly what Job's friend Elihu has been saying since chapter 36. 'Don't expect to understand God,' Elihu says, 'just fear him' (37.24). But the problem is that he isn't following his own advice. He is still trying to give a neat, pre-packaged theory about God, rather than facing the enormity of God himself. And Jesus's disciples are as afraid of the end of the storm as of the storm itself, because it has brought them up sharply against God. The Corinthians, Paul says, have reservations about him and his ministry. Is it because they do not like the raw, unavoidable presence of God in the preaching of Paul?

'Give us the theory,' human beings cry out to God, 'but don't give us yourself. That's more than we want.' This then, is the power of God, the huge generosity that fills our little outstretched begging bowls so full that the bowl is utterly swept away in the torrent. Is that more than you bargained for?

In his beautifully honest and humble book *Basil in Blunderland* the late Cardinal Hume says that for years he lived with a concept of God as a kind of gigantic teacher or policeman, who would know if you sneaked into the larder and took an apple, and would make sure you paid for it. 'Now many years later', he writes, 'I have an idea that God would have said to the small boy, "Take two . . .".'[1]

So the end of the story of Job is that Job – the devout and lifelong servant of God – says to him, 'I had no idea. I had only heard about you before, but now I've seen you, I know I can only throw myself on your mercy' (42.5, 6). The disciples, too, have to learn to trust God for what God is and gives and not for what they would like. As they argue with Jesus and try to dissuade him from the road to the cross, do their hearts cling to that moment when he stilled the storm? 'More of that,' they cry, forgetting that they were afraid of it when they saw it. This is a lesson that Paul has amply learned – the thrilling, mad power of God, recklessly throwing out apples, and bread to the starving. Will the Corinthians open their hearts to it, or we ours? Or do we actually feel safer with a world that will stingily dole out one apple and make sure we pay for it?

---

[1] *Basil in Blunderland*, DLT, 1997.

Proper 8

———— ⌇ ————

Wisdom of Solomon 1.13–15; 2.23, 24
2 Corinthians 8.7–15
Mark 5.21–43

'Do not fear, only believe,' Jesus says to Jairus. It's easier said than done, of course, with his daughter dead and the house full of the sound of wailing mourners. It's also quite ironic, in that it is fear of just this moment that has driven Jairus to Jesus in the first place.

Both of the people Jesus encounters in today's Gospel reading are driven by one kind of fear so strongly that it overcomes all kinds of other fears that they might be expected to feel. Jairus's overwhelming fear is that his daughter will die. Mark's storytelling never wastes words, but he doesn't need to describe how much Jairus loves his daughter. His actions make it crystal clear. He is risking the disapproval of his community, in which he is a leading figure; he is pushing aside his own inevitable doubts and uncertainties about who Jesus is and by what power he performs healings. He is prepared to risk everything for the faint hope of life for his daughter. So he elbows his way to the front of the whispering, nudging crowd, and makes his demand of Jesus. And Jesus goes with him. No words said, no questions asked.

The nameless woman, too, has one fierce fear that puts all the others in the shade. Her fear is that she will never be well again, she will always be bone-tired, pale, thin, listless and in pain. But also, she will always be alone, never fully part of the community, no one to help her bear her condition more cheerfully. So she braves the fear of discovery and rejection by the crowd, the fear of painful, embarrassing exposure if the bandages and extra clothes she has bound around herself do not hold, the fear that she will not reach Jesus through the crowds, or that if she does, it will be useless.

You can tell that her driving fear is long-term, that she has lived with it for so long that it has changed her character completely. Once, presumably, she was reasonably well-off – comfortable enough, at any rate, to afford a lot of doctors, and confident enough to go on spending her money in expectation of a cure. But now she is poor and cowed and tired. She is not like Jairus who, even in the extremity of his fear, is a man of authority who expects to be heard and to get his own way. This woman is not even intending to ask for what she needs because she is sure the answer would be no. But she has just enough desperation left to try to steal it.

Her chance comes as the crowd begins to move. Jesus and Jairus are walking fast to get to the sick child, and the crowd is streaming around them, thinner in some places where people are not hurrying to be at the front. The woman seizes her chance, while the important men are concentrating on their important things. She reaches out her hand and brushes Jesus's clothes as they blow out behind him with the speed of his walking. She had meant to turn away at once and hobble off home and wait and hope, but she is shocked into stillness by her body's reaction. How long is it since she felt well? So long that she can hardly recognize the feeling. And in that one awed moment, the crowd stops moving and she hears the dreadful question, 'Who touched me?'

She could have stood silent, but part of her needs the crowd to see what has happened to her, to make it real, to assure her that she isn't imagining it, even if she gets into terrible trouble. It is strange to have all those eyes on her, when she has spent years with eyes that avoided her or slid away from her fast. Most of the eyes are not friendly. She is just a distraction, kneeling there, abject and shaking. The crowd wants to get on to Jairus's house to see the real drama unfold. They expect Jesus to push her away, perhaps even to make her ill again. Instead, he tells her that she has done right, and that her health is what she deserves and has won for herself.

Jairus must be in an agony of impatience while all of this is going on. He knows that every second counts and, sure enough, when they get home at last, it is too late. Even in the midst of his terrible grief, he can spare a little hatred for the insignificant woman whose healing has cost him his daughter.

Don't be afraid, Jesus says. God's love is not that small. There is enough for the woman and your daughter. There is enough for all.

Proper 9

—— ❧ ——

Ezekiel 2.1–5
2 Corinthians 12.2–10
Mark 6.1–13

This passage of 2 Corinthians has caused enormous speculation down the ages. It is tantalisingly full of hints about Paul, which may have made sense to his readers but which we can only fill out with hyperactive imaginings, which can never be proved or disproved. It seems pretty certain that Paul is talking about his own spiritual experience in the first half of chapter 12. The convoluted language and the use of the third person shows how reluctant he is to do so, but he is driven to it by the theological point he has to make. For some people, this kind of mystical experience is a 'natural' result of meeting with God. It clearly was for Paul, as his encounter with Jesus on the road to Damascus shows. And does Galatians hint at a prolonged period of spiritual experience, in the three years after Paul's conversion, before his Gentile ministry begins (Galatians 1.17–18)? But the point Paul is making to the Corinthians is that these experiences are irrelevant – it is the meeting with God that matters, not the form it takes. The Corinthians are rather keen on exciting experiences, and they have clearly been intrigued by 'super-apostles' (2 Corinthians 11.5), who have, presumably, been pandering to their love of spectacle. So Paul needs to make it clear that he is not talking out of envy of those who have experiences that he doesn't. He could match them in every way. But his calling as an apostle is not to gather crowds of admiring followers who gasp at his spiritual prowess. His calling is to witness to Christ.

But if we long, like the Corinthians, to know exactly what Paul means by being 'caught up into Paradise', we also long, tabloid readers that we are, to know what his 'thorn in the flesh' was. We want to know the highs and the lows. Some commentators have assumed that Paul's 'thorn' was a physical defect of some kind. But the context makes it just as likely that the 'thorn' is actually someone who is opposing and undermining Paul's work. These 'super-apostles' have been bringing out the worst in Paul, making him defensive, aggressive, boastful, suggesting that his gospel is not the real one, dividing the community he loves and has struggled over. He has begged God three times to remove this obstacle, but God has said no.

If that is a correct interpretation of the situation, then God's 'No' to Paul is a very hard thing to hear. God's 'No' means that Paul must live without God's public vindication of his apostleship. It also means that Paul has to hear God's deeper challenge. 'Do you want to be proved right for my sake, or for your own?' We can all too easily convince ourselves that unless we are publicly proved right, God will be miserable. But that is simply not true. God does not need popular acclamation to know that he is right. He is not dependent upon the world's good opinion. That is our problem. God is our God and our saviour, whatever opinion polls may say, and he knows it. We don't actually need to worry about God. So whatever Paul's thorn in the flesh is, it is something that reminds him of that basic fact. It is something that, at least in Paul's own view, makes him less plausible and authoritative for God. But that is why it is God's gift to him, because it reminds him that Paul is dependent upon God, not vice versa.

It is not wrong to long for love and support and understanding. But those things, like mystical experiences, are the occasional luxuries, rather than the staple fare of Christians. When Jesus goes home, with his disciples, does he hope to be able to relax among people who love and trust him? If so, he is sorely disappointed. His people resent his authority, his reputation, his followers. They want to pull him back down to their level. They don't want to face the challenge and the opportunity that he brings. They spend all their efforts on looking for reasons not to pay attention to him. The question, 'Who does he think he is?' frees them from the responsibility of hearing what he is saying. But if Jesus is shocked by them, and if they reinforce his sense of loneliness and isolation, that does not deter him from doing the will of the Father. Instinctively, at a time when his own authority is called into question by the disbelief of his townspeople, he looks around for another way, and sends his disciples out to preach. That is the vital thing for him – not that people love and honour him, but that God's word is heard and his will is done.

Proper 10

———— ≈ ————

Amos 7.7–15
Ephesians 1.3–14
Mark 6.14–29

The letter to the Ephesians sets the life of the Christian Church in the context of the cosmic plan of God. The letter will go on to give quite detailed advice about how Christians should live together, day to day, but it is important that that advice should be seen in its proper setting. Christianity is not, at its heart, about living a decent and moral life. It is about living the life we were created for, in tune with the God who made us. That is why Christians are right to agonize over the way our lives bear witness to the God we seek and serve. We are trying to brush away the dust and dirt that cover the beloved features, not bury them even deeper. Luckily, our frantic but ineffectual efforts are not the only force at work. Behind them all is the awesome majesty of God, whose purposes will not be thwarted, even though, dog-like, our digging obscures more than it reveals.

So Ephesians begins right at the very beginning, reminding the reader of our dependence upon God, and how much we already have to thank him for. In Christ, God has always chosen to be our God. Even before we existed, and certainly before we consciously turned towards God, God chooses that we are to be 'in Christ', and share that relationship between Father and Son. It is the nature of God the Son to go out and show the love of the Father, so that Son and Spirit can gather everything that is made back into the life of the maker (v. 10). This is what we are made for. We are designed to be part of the ceaseless flow of love between Father, Son and Holy Spirit.

Christians, then, live as people who know God's plan for the world. We know that God has made us to be part of his glorious life and love. We carry in our very blood the serum, the antidote to the belief that life is pointless and that evil always triumphs. Our baptism, you might say, injects us with the Holy Spirit so that now, inseparably linked with our own weary, bored, unbelieving life-blood is the life-blood of God, who creates, sustains and redeems all things. And the life of God is irresistible, as Jesus's resurrection shows.

We do need to make it our solemn and binding duty never to forget the Christian calling to joy and hope, to praising and glorifying our God. We do need to hold always before us the knowledge that the world and its fate are in God's hands, and he who has held it in love from its birth is not going to drop it now. Knowing the huge and final plan of God does not always help us to see where we are going every day. Many, many days and weeks and months can pass without any sign that they are furthering the final goal of gathering the world into Christ. Most of our own plans are all too clearly human and lead, if we are lucky, into the dust and, if we are not so lucky, into apparent disaster.

As John the Baptist waited to have his head chopped off, did he believe that things were still on track and leading to God's goals? It can't have been at all obvious. He'd been sitting in prison for some time, visited regularly by Herod. Perhaps John believed that he was beginning to get through to Herod, beginning to make him see that he was leading a life that was contrary to the will of God. And then one rash promise from Herod, and John is dead, and the opportunity gone. If, as Mark suggests, Herod continued to feel guilty about John's death, still it had no visible effect upon his future behaviour. We readers of the Gospel know the central role John the Baptist plays as God's herald to the coming Son, and so we also need to note that John did exactly what he was supposed to do, and yet it did not bring him fame, fortune and friends. John fulfils his role by standing aside, making room for the Son, and continuing to bear faithful witness right up to his strange and tragic end.

To praise and glorify God, and to live in the truthful knowledge of the overriding purposes of God will not necessarily make our lives easy. As followers of Christ, the crucified and risen Lord, the image of the invisible God and the fulfilment of all of God's plans, we should perhaps not be surprised by that.

Proper 11

———— ∽ ————

Jeremiah 23.1–6
Ephesians 2.11–22
Mark 6.30–34, 53–56

In today's reading from Mark's Gospel, we get a strong sense of the enormous pressure Jesus and the disciples were under at this point in his ministry. Jesus is at the height of his popularity and although his conflict with the religious authorities has begun, as chapters 2 and 3 make clear, it has not yet escalated into full public confrontation. To the crowds who follow him everywhere he goes, Jesus is still a teacher and healer, not primarily a political player. Jesus knows this about them. He knows that they come to him for immediate gratification and to satisfy their pressing need. Just like sheep, they have no long-term plans. Sheep don't worry about what will happen when they have eaten all the grass in their field, or when winter comes. That's the job of the shepherd. In the same way, the people who flock round Jesus have come either just for entertainment or for healing, but without any idea that what Jesus is offering has more long-term consequences than either of those things. That's what he sees, as he looks at them: he sees sheep with no shepherd and, we are told, he 'began to teach them many things' – not make decisions for them, like their shepherd, but teach them things so that they can be human beings, not sheep any more.

What makes Jesus's compassion and understanding for the crowds even more striking are the circumstances in which all of this is taking place. His disciples have just come back from a groundbreaking independent mission and are longing to tell him all about it. They are all tired out, every conversation they have is interrupted, they are recognized and tracked wherever they go, they are not eating or sleeping properly. All of them must be aware that they are living on their nerves and their instincts. Clearly, in that utterly defenceless state, Jesus's instincts are to put others and their needs first. We rightly concentrate on the cross when we are thinking about what Jesus suffered in order to bring about our salvation, but this passage reminds us that Jesus's bodily existence does not begin and end on the cross. Many of us who hope and pray that we will never be called upon to suffer as he did on the cross can remember that he also suffered from hunger, weariness, stress and all the more common symptoms of embodied living.

Is it accidental that Ephesians puts so much emphasis on the bodiliness of the way in which our salvation was achieved? Ephesians 2.14 does not say, as you might expect, that Jesus's physical suffering on the cross wins our salvation. Instead, it says that his 'fleshliness', in and of itself, unites the divided and breaks down the walls of hostility. All the metaphors of belonging and wholeness that are used in verses 19–22 depend on this work done by Jesus in the flesh. Because Jesus came in the flesh, we are now familiar and beloved to each other, instead of unrecognized and untrustworthy. Because Jesus came in the flesh, we are now part of God's family. Because Jesus came in the flesh, we can, together, be built up into the place where God lives on earth, where he may be visited and worshipped and known. Because Jesus came in the flesh, our bodies are familiar with the Holy Spirit and, through him, with the Father.

It is so tempting to spiritualize salvation, but the Christian gospel of incarnation absolutely militates against that. God himself has made our bodiliness central to salvation. If we will not be saved in and through our actual, physical lives, we will not be saved by Christ at all. That is why this terrible, painful, costly debate that is going on in the Anglican Church now about the proper use of sexuality is, at least in its subject matter, necessary. It does matter what we do with our bodies. We are right to sense, however inarticulately, that something vital is at issue here. We may be wrong to think that it all hinges on our bodies seen in sexual terms. We may be wilfully ignoring the other facts about being embodied creatures, like the fact that many of us struggle with obesity while others starve, or the fact that bodies with different coloured skins are treated differently, or the fact that all bodies are born to die. All of these are truths about being creatures whose embodied existence Jesus chose to share in order to break down walls of hostility between us. The only way in which these our bodies can be built up into the temple of God is if we will hold hands and stand, body to body, together.

Proper 12

———— ❧ ————

2 Kings 4.42–44
Ephesians 3.14–21
John 6.1–21

The story of the feeding of the five thousand is found in all four Gospels, making it one of the best attested of Jesus's miracles. John's Gospel sometimes uses memories and stories that clearly come from different sources from the ones used by the other three Gospels. So this episode of miraculous feeding must be one that was told in pretty well all the early Christian witness to Jesus. It might very well have been regularly retold in a eucharistic setting, as the way Jesus breaks the bread and gives thanks would be a good way into teaching about the eucharistic meal, and Jesus's self-breaking on the cross. But there are also details that are particular and superfluous to that teaching use, that make it clear that this is a real memory of an extraordinary event. For example, the little boy and his fish – I can't help feeling that the boy may have had some role in keeping the story fresh. We aren't told who he was, but it is slightly odd that in such a huge crowd of people, the disciples knew he was there and that he had his picnic with him. Perhaps he was even the son of one of the disciples, or one of Jesus's regular followers. Or perhaps he was just a very loud and ubiquitous boy, the sort you can't help noticing in any crowd. Either way, I'm sure he was often called upon in later life to tell the story of what happened when Jesus took his sandwiches.

St John, always the theologian, and clearly with high expecta-tions of the intelligence of his readership, puts the feeding miracle in the context of Passover. What God is doing in Jesus is similar to the divine action that brought the people of Israel safely out of Egypt. But he also expects his readers to understand that God's new act of power is only prefigured in the feeding of the five thousand. It is to come to its full fruition in the cross, when Jesus breaks himself to nourish the whole world. So John's readers should groan with despair as they hear that people respond to this miracle by trying to make Jesus King. The crowds are already obsessed with Jesus's miracles. They have followed him to see healings and signs, and now they have been rewarded for their persistence by another demonstration of magic. The conclusions they draw are both truthful and perverse. They assume, rightly, that here is God's chosen Messiah, but they have no idea how the Messiah will bring God's salvation. They have seen the power and wholly misunderstood it while we, thanks to John, can see its real meaning. That they are correct in their assumptions about who Jesus is is immediately reinforced by the story of the stilling of the storm and the walking on the water. Jesus is, indeed, the one who brings the power and presence of God. The creation obeys him through whom it was made – unlike us.

Learning to respond to our creator is what this passage in Ephesians is all about. To be 'rooted and grounded' (v. 17) in the love of Christ is to come back to the source of our life. It is God who makes us, with care and individuality, not just in a great and indiscriminate creative splurge, but each one given its name, its particularity. As we gradually learn to breathe the air of the Holy Spirit, filling our lungs with it, so we learn what the wind and the waves knew instinctively: that we are made to respond to God. Everywhere we look, we see the power of God at work, in all that he has made and remade and in all that he has done and is doing.

Christian praying and believing can be very small and unimaginative, as though we don't really think God can manage more than the three wishes of so many fairy tales. We need to hoard our wishes, and make sure we only ask for what we really want and don't waste the magical power. But Ephesians says, 'Don't be so silly.' It constantly widens the frame, so that our lives are put in the context of God the creator and redeemer of the world. Part of us is terrified of that power, as the disciples were terrified when they saw Jesus walking towards them on the water. If that creative power, the power of God's unimaginable love, is unleashed on the world and, even more frighteningly, is at work in us, then we are adrift beyond our limits. If we have to see the world with that shatteringly generous love, then we, and the world, will be irrevocably changed. It is not ours to control, but we could co-operate.

Proper 13

——— ❧ ———

Exodus 16.2–4, 9–15
Ephesians 4.1–16
John 6.24–35

This is a very revealing set of questions and answers between Jesus and the people following him. It tells us a lot about what the people thought they were looking for in Jesus, and gives us one of Jesus's own central definitions of his work.

The theme is food, which is not surprising, considering the conversation follows very closely on the feeding of the five thousand. At the beginning of chapter 6, we are told that the people following Jesus are hoping for more healing miracles, but now, after being fed by him, they are hoping never to go without a meal again. They are quite indignant with him for slipping away, and very relieved to have caught up with him again.

We don't know very much about the people who followed Jesus. They can't have had steady nine-to-five kind of jobs, because some of them obviously followed him around for days. Perhaps they were very largely from the strand of society where the source of the next meal is a continual worry. Jesus doesn't seem to be angry with them, but he is definitely trying to make them look beyond lunch time. For many of them, this conversation is to be a turning point. Up to now they have been largely spectators and recipients, but Jesus is forcing them to think and make choices. They have followed, watched, eaten and had a really exciting time, and most of them hope it will continue. But now they are confronted with the annoying question of meaning. What do Jesus's signs and miracles tell us? By the end of this chapter of the Gospel, quite a lot of the crowd will have gone home, unwilling or unable to answer that question satisfactorily.

To begin with, they humour Jesus, though carefully skirting round the central issue. Although Jesus challenges them not to waste time on things that have no lasting value, he instantly ties that in with his own mission. 'Oh, right,' they say, 'we're on to religion. OK, so tell us about your idea of God, then.' They have sort of noticed that Jesus means them to ask about who this 'Son of Man' is, but they're not sure that they want to know the answer. But Jesus presses again. This is no abstract theological discussion from which everyone can go home with their ideas unchanged. This requires a commitment, now, to Jesus.

The people try to wriggle out of it. 'Do another miracle to help us believe,' they say. And remember, these are people who have just the day before seen Jesus feed five thousand people with five loaves and two fishes. This request could hardly be more cheeky. But Jesus will not let them pretend that they have not understood. He will not let them go home and talk only about the amazing things they have seen. Jesus's mission is not a spectator sport. 'I am the bread of life,' he says bluntly. 'Do you want it, or not?' He completely cuts across all their attempts to stop him from demanding a decision.

Isn't it strange that they don't know how to answer? When they could persuade themselves that Jesus was only talking about actual food, they knew the answer quickly enough. 'Give it to us always!' they say. But now, when it is clear what Jesus is really talking about, the crowd go quiet. They know they don't want to go hungry again, but they don't know if they want salvation.

It is terribly important to know that, about our deepest needs and desires, we can be remarkably stupid. According to Ephesians, it is one of the functions of the Church to minimize that stupidity. There is always the hope that if we stick together, somebody else will know what you don't and vice versa. Otherwise you are in danger of being as stupid as a single arm, out there on its own, thinking it can function fully. This metaphor of the Church as a body is not the only description in the New Testament of the nature of the Christian community, though it is one of the most vivid. Pretty well all the descriptions, though, have unity as one of their central themes. Unfortunately, we don't seem to have taken that in. Our natural stupidity, that doesn't know any more than that we need lunch for today and tomorrow, reasserts itself. If our salvation depends upon being one body, indwelled by the Holy Spirit, activated by Christ the head, do we want it or not? Or would we rather be the perfect arm, utterly divorced from the body, therefore utterly useless, but nonetheless proudly uncompromised by trying to live with people who are different? If Ephesians is right, that's the choice. Take it or leave it.

Proper 14

—— ~ ——

1 Kings 19.4–8
Ephesians 4.25—5.2
John 6.35, 41–51

On the grounds that there is no point in telling someone to do something if they are already doing it, the Ephesian community must be quite like a church you know well. It is interesting how much of this section is concerned with *talk*. There is a rather perfunctory mention, in verse 28, that thieving is wrong, but even that is condemned, in this context, because it is an activity destructive of community, rather than because it is innately wrong. (It clearly is, I hasten to add, but that is not the point that is being made here.)

So, apparently, the chief threat to the internal harmony of the Ephesian community is talk. Lying and anger are the main forms of talk that are destabilizing the Ephesian church, and verse 31 details the different forms that these emotions can have, while verse 32 suggests countermeasures.

But the real point of the section comes in the last verse of chapter 4 and the first two verses of chapter 5. The well-being of the Christian community is not just important because it will make us happier, or better able to market our brand product because of our excellent record for keeping our employees happy. It's more that, if we cannot build strong community, there is no point in us at all. We demonstrate that we do not understand God, and so completely undermine our witness to him, Ephesians suggests. We are called together to live as 'imitators of God'. We have come, through the gracious and costly work of God the Son, to know the Father, and to know that we are his children too. Our life together shows our family likeness, and so enables others to begin to see what God is like. That is why actions of ours that damage our common life 'grieve the Holy Spirit', whose task and goal it is to build us into the likeness of the Son, so that we too can love the Father.

Ephesians does not tell us what we are to do in cases of deep and genuine disagreement. But given this very high theology of Chris-

96

tian community, it is unlikely that it would take schism as anything but the most serious possible failure. What else is said to 'grieve the Holy Spirit'? To give ourselves up for one another marks us as imitators of Christ, and Christ certainly managed to do this without needing everyone to agree with him first, and admit he was right.

Although the reference in Ephesians to Christ's self-giving almost certainly refers to the cross, John's Gospel makes it poignantly clear how much else, day to day, was involved in that whole movement of self-giving, through incarnation to death and resurrection. Living constantly with those who misunderstand and misjudge is part of the daily fate of the incarnate Son of God. Here in chapter 6, Jesus is speaking vividly and with force about what he has come for, and yet people misunderstand him. It is more than honest perplexity, in some cases. It is almost as though there is a wilful determination not to understand. 'Who does he think he is?' is basically what people are asking.

Patiently, Jesus tries to explain, as he does so often in John's Gospel, that he is not making claims for himself, but simply building on what they already should know about God. God has been working, Father, Son and Holy Spirit, from our creation, to make our hearts warm to the Son incarnate, just as God has been working, from our creation, to bring us to share in his life. What Jesus is offering is something that we should instinctively recognize, which is the source of our true life.

But built into Jesus's glorious offer of himself as the bread of life is the knowledge that we will not recognize it, that we will turn away from it and choose dust and ashes and death. There is bitter irony in these words 'bread', 'life', 'flesh'. Since, wilfully and stubbornly, we choose death, rather than the life that we were made for, Jesus, with painful but irrepressible creativity, chooses death too. He chooses to be in our death, so that even as we choose death, we choose him. There is no illusion in Jesus's choice to be the bread of our life.

Why does God make this extraordinary choice? Why does he give us the power to crucify the Son, to continue, even after the death and resurrection, to grieve the Holy Spirit by our obtuse unwillingness to acknowledge our dependence upon God and upon each other? God does not need us, since he is complete in himself, Father, Son and Spirit. But perhaps it is this sheer gratuity and grace that we find most incomprehensible about God.

Proper 15

—— ∽ ——

Proverbs 9.1–6
Ephesians 5.15–20
John 6.51–58

'You are what you eat', so the saying goes. Our modern western culture is wise to the fact that food is not all the same, and will not all be good for you. We are now very anxious about food additives, very aware of possible allergies to food that might normally be thought nutritious. We spend a lot of time worrying, rather literally, about where the next meal is coming from. Was it organically grown? Did it start life too near a motorway? Will its deceptive rosiness mask the slow pollutants it contains? Not all cultures have quite that luxury. Our children have food fads, sometimes encouraged by us, in case of allergic reactions, but some children suck helplessly at empty paps, or scavenge the streets for almost anything that will fill the aching void in their bellies. Their version might be, 'You are *if* you eat.' We who pick and choose and read every detail of our supermarket labels still showed a tendency to be shocked when an African country recently refused food aid if it had been genetically modified. In every culture and at every time, food has been one of the main obsessions of human beings, though we might be unusual in the West in being a culture obsessed with not eating, rather than eating.

The Jewish culture into which Jesus spoke was particularly sensitive to issues of food. They already knew that their God was very interested in food. This was shown not just by the rituals and taboos surrounding food preparation, but also by a whole host of other things. The people of Israel knew that God had himself provided food for them in the desert, when they were about to starve. They knew that for certain of his servants, like Elijah the Tishbite, God sent his creatures to bring them food. They knew that food had been the cause of their separation from God, as Adam and Eve ate the apple, and that food, as symbolized by the Passover meal, set them apart as the people whom God himself chose and brought out of slavery.

Jesus's eating habits were already causing some comment. He was not an ascetic like John the Baptist, and he was known to be a little indiscriminating in who he ate with (Mark 2.15ff., for example). For a people like this, the teaching of a religious leader about food would be part of how they assessed his message. So their suspicions are already slightly raised before Jesus says this particularly disgusting and outrageous thing. We who are used to reading Jesus's words as reference to the eucharist may not hear the full and shocking impact of what he says. But John's Gospel makes it completely clear that his words caused major ripples, and lost him some followers.

Their disgust and bewilderment are understandable, if you read the words as though you did not know the future history of the Church. It sounds as though Jesus is talking about violent cannibalism. Indeed, early Christians were, half-seriously, accused of cannibalism in later years, by those who heard that their central ritual involved eating flesh and drinking blood.

Unquestionably, Jesus intended to shock. The violence of his words is calculated. Throughout this chapter he has been involved in conversations with people who do not want to see what he is talking about. They are happy with his miracles. They are quite intrigued by some of his teaching, but they are still assuming that, basically, they choose. They decide whether or not he is religiously interesting and important. They tack on the bits of his teaching that they like to the system that they already live with. They come and listen when it suits them, and go back to their ordinary lives when they need to. But Jesus is not an optional extra. Jesus is life, the only possible source of it. Feeding on Jesus is our only hope. The world in which we depend upon other kinds of food is not the real world. The real world is fed only by Jesus, created in him, redeemed by him and sustained through him alone. We live wholly dependent upon the life of Jesus, which is the life of God, the source of all life.

How can Jesus make the people understand this, when they persist in seeing him as one of a number of possible options? His words are meant to force a reaction, then and now. We may be Christians, but do we actually believe, any more than Jesus's original hearers did, that 'unless you eat the flesh of the Son of Man and drink his blood, you have no life in you'? Or do we persist in choosing the bread which can only sustain the illusion of life?

Proper 16

———— ~ ————

Joshua 24.1–2a, 14–18
Ephesians 6.10–20
John 6.56–69

Peter's tale:

That's about the only time I ever remember being sure that I'd got it right. Oh, I don't mean that I had doubts about what came out of my mouth when I was preaching to people after the Lord had risen. But those words never really felt like mine. I remember Jesus saying that the Spirit would come and give us the words, and that has certainly been my experience. When I stand up to witness to what I have seen and heard, I know I am doing it through a power that isn't my own. That doesn't mean that I always get it right, or even that I always make myself clear, but I do get the sense that the responsibility lies elsewhere. I have to do my best, and then leave the consequences up to the Lord.

And I don't mean to be all modest when I say that's the only time I got it right on my own. I've never been shy, and I don't mind making a fool of myself. My mother said I started talking almost as soon as I got out of the womb, and I haven't stopped since! When I'm nervous or excited or happy or sad or drunk or sober – I talk. All the others used to rely on me to start the ball rolling. I'd say something daft to Jesus, and then they could come in sounding judicious and sensible when they'd had a chance to see how he reacted to what I said. I didn't mind. Every group needs someone like me, and even if people do sometimes think I'm an idiot, they usually like me too. Jesus did tell me off once or twice, when I was really crass, but on the whole he was pleased that I wasn't too scared to risk things. The others never liked to ask him what he was doing, or what his mission was, but I just jumped in with both feet and told him straight out that I thought he was the Messiah. I knew all the others wanted to find out whether or not he was, but didn't dare ask. Of course, I realize now how little I understood what it means to be God's Messiah, but I was sort of right about Jesus anyway, wasn't I?

But the time I'm trying to tell you about was odd. We'd had a real rollercoaster few days. Jesus was doing the kind of miracles that make your hair stand up on the nape of your neck with a mixture of excitement and fear. He was healing people, and feeding thousands of people with hardly anything, and then there was that time when he came walking to us across the water – I'll never forget it, and I still can't describe, to this day, what it looked like, to see him *walking* on the water towards us. We hardly had any time together to talk things over because hordes of wildly excited people were following us everywhere, begging for more.

But then, suddenly, they started turning nasty. Jesus tried to talk to them, and explain what he was up to and who he was, and they hated it. They didn't understand – well, to be honest, neither did we. He kept telling us that he had to die and we had to eat him if we were to live with him in the life of God. That sounded mad and thoroughly disgusting as well. We all felt that he wasn't explaining himself at all well, and that he was deliberately putting people off, just when he was getting a real following. I still wonder if that was actually part of what he was trying to do. Perhaps he actually wanted to get rid of all those people who were determined to believe he was what they wanted him to be, and weren't prepared to listen and find out what he thought he was himself.

Anyway, that was certainly the effect he had. Lots of people stopped travelling with us that day, and stopped thinking of themselves as followers of Jesus. He'd made it just too hard for them. But even if that was what he'd expected, he was sad. I remember he turned to those of us who were left and said, 'Do you want to go, too? It isn't going to get any easier, you know. In fact, it's going to get much harder. If you think this is difficult to understand, you just wait. Why don't you go now, while the going's good?'

And that's when I said it.

'Where else could we go? You're the only one who can speak the words of life.'

I knew I was right, as I said the words, and I know it to this day.

Proper 17

———— ∿ ————

Deuteronomy 4.1–2, 6–9
James 1.17–27
Mark 7.1–8, 14, 15, 21–23

We rather value versatility and unpredictability in people. To say that someone is predictable is to imply that they are boring and hidebound. I suspect that this actually reflects the comparative security and dependability of a lot of our lives in the West. Most of us know where our next meal is coming from, when our next holiday will be, even quite accurately when our next baby will be born. We can afford the luxury of finding predictability boring. But that is still not the case for most of the world. Unpredictable weather can spell death, and an unplanned pregnancy starvation. No wonder that many cultures value God's immutability so highly. Even we, who think we like variety, may actually be unexpectedly hurt by friends or partners who leave us for someone new and more exciting. We say that they have acted out of character, when before we might have thought we found their whimsicality appealing. Or we travel in search of novelty and then recreate our own home wherever we go. Perhaps we are not entirely truthful with ourselves in thinking that stability is tedious. 'Yesterday, today, for ever, Jesus is the same. All may change, but Jesus never, glory to his name,' runs the chorus that has comforted many for years.

These verses from James are verses in praise of unchangingness. In God there is no change. Things from outside him cannot make God react uncharacteristically. Light does not force strange shadows from him, making him appear what he is not. God does not have to return to the drawing board each morning with his design and alter it to fit unpredicted events, and we cannot force God's hand by shouting at him.

But if this kind of language quickly degenerates into a description of God's master plan which seems to leave no space for genuine human freedom, read the rest of what James says in this chapter. He is not saying that God has a kind of gigantic crystal ball in which he has already seen everything that will ever be. Nor is he saying that we are just pieces on a celestial chessboard, destined to move only according to the rules. What he is actually saying is that nothing – nothing – nothing can make God act in a way that is not characteristic. God is so completely himself, at home with himself, at ease with himself, that he has the genuine freedom to be who he is, always. He is not trying to change to get affection or a laugh or more power. God is wholly, dynamically content. And if that sounds like a contradiction in terms, just think of the one or two genuinely happy people you know. The late, great, Metropolitan Anthony of Sourozh, for example, radiated a kind of energetic contentment that made everyone he was with feel more content to be themselves, and more determined to be better. Could that be, perhaps, a pale reflection of the nature of God?

Much modern Christian writing has misunderstood what is meant by the immutability of God, and has assumed that it makes God less loving, less personal, less like Jesus. But perhaps, in fact, God's unchangingness is a sign that God does not need to waste time worrying about himself at all, and so is wholly available, wholly present for us, in a way that no human being can ever be; because for us, some part of our own worry or insecurity always impinges, to a greater or lesser degree.

James is here exhorting us to imitate God in knowing what we are like. Unlike God, we may need to change, but even this cannot be done if we do not really know ourselves in the first place. We can, he says, know ourselves in a completely superficial way, so that we might recognize ourselves if glimpsed in a mirror, without having any idea of how we behave, or how others perceive us. Instead of looking into the mirror, we have to look, James suggests, into the steadfast nature of God, and begin to see ourselves truly. Slowly, slowly, as we get to know ourselves through God's eyes, our lives will become consistent with the great and liberating consistency of God. We will not have to vow each morning to behave with love and charity because love and charity will be what we are. At the moment they are still attributes that we can sometimes summon up and sometimes not, depending what kind of mood we are in. We need to work towards that perfect state that we see in the nature of God, where doing and being are never separated.

Proper 18

——— ⁓ ———

Isaiah 35.4–7a
James 2.1–17
Mark 7.24–37

I suppose it's comforting, in an Eeyore-ish kind of way, to know that ours is not the only generation of Christians to think that belief is simply a matter of the words you use, and that it doesn't need to affect ordinary life in any way. James is writing to a Christian church that is, apparently, just like ours. The people who go to James's church are convinced enough of the claims of the gospel to call themselves Christians, and to meet regularly with others. But they don't see this as a matter that affects their fundamental understanding of the structuring of the universe. James finds this almost incredible.

His readers seem to be viewing faith as a kind of insurance policy: you probably need it as part of a sensible attempt to keep unpleasant reality at bay; in case of sickness or accident, it's nice to know that God is on your side. And surely part of the point of an insurance policy is that it allows you to carry on your normal life without any worries about the consequences of your actions? So James's congregation still like rich people better than poor people, clean people better than dirty people, well people better than sick people because, after all, who doesn't?

God doesn't, is James's alarming answer. God doesn't have favourites. God is shockingly blind to the normal measures of society. He doesn't seem to notice accents, or cost out people's clothes and treat them accordingly. He has absolutely no need to keep in with the rich and famous, or to find favour with the influential. After all, he is God.

One of the worrying consequences of this is the possibility that God doesn't realize where he belongs in our carefully planned life. He might not be aware that he is a fail-safe mechanism, to be invoked when we are up against something that we can't cope with on our own. He might, indeed, believe that he is the way, the truth and the life, and that our attempts to make him fit our way, our truth and our life are at best touchingly misplaced and at worst completely absurd.

Faith changes the way you live, James says, in that obnoxiously black and white way of his. You might feel tempted, at this point, to turn to that nice St Paul, who really understands about the importance of faith, and doesn't go droning on about having to do things as well. Dream on. Try reading Romans 6. There is no escaping the New Testament conviction that faith is a commitment to a changed way of life, because it is a commitment to trying to see the world with the eyes of God. This has enormous benefits for us personally, since God is understanding and forgiving beyond what we could ever expect or deserve. But the downside is that he is equally concerned about others. We are not his favourites. We must try to see as we are seen, James says in verse 13. We cannot expect God to use one standard of judgement on us if that is not the standard of judgement that we are using on anyone else.

Probably, however, we should give ourselves permission not always to be certain of God's standards. There are some fairly consistent clues in the New Testament and, sadly, suspicion of the lure of wealth is one of them. But there is also the fascinating story we have in Mark's Gospel, of Jesus's own vision being enlarged by his encounter with the Syro-Phoenician woman. It feels shocking to say that this woman, in her insistent need, reminded the Son of the scope of the Father's love. But the very least the story demands is to see Jesus deeply moved by the depths of the woman's faith. She is certain that God does not have favourites, and that there is always enough in his provision to go round. It is we who are stingy, not God.

Over and over again the Gospels show us Jesus interacting with those whom most societies consider marginal. Today it might be a woman who is also a gentile, and a deaf man who cannot communicate, but most of the stories are the same. They suggest that there is something about being an insider, comfortable in the world you live in, that actually makes it harder to hear God. If the world is basically treating you quite benignly, then you tend to forget that its standards may not be God's. Why would you want to be reminded of something that might end up making your life more uncomfortable?

When James says, 'beware of a faith that has not visibly changed your life', he is speaking words we have to hear, but seldom want to.

Proper 19

—— ∼ ——

Isaiah 50.4–9a
James 3.1–12
Mark 8.27–38

The disciples are quite enjoying the discussion, to begin with. Everywhere they've been with Jesus, they have heard speculation. People must have asked them, over and over again, 'Who is your master? Where does he get his power from? What's he really up to?' The disciples are very tactful. They only pass on the repeatable theories they have heard. They don't say, 'Some people think you're mad, and some people think you're demon-possessed, and some people think you're a revolutionary.' No, they stick to the complimentary and religious options. They do this partly to be kind to Jesus, but partly also for their own sakes. After all, if they're his followers, they are going to be tarred with the same brush as him.

It's very easy, passing on the gossip. Lots of voices are raised with contributions to the conversation. But when Jesus asks the next question, there is sudden silence. The next question is going to commit the one who answers it. It might make him look stupid, if he gets it wrong; it might make him look overcommitted or undercommitted to Jesus. Suppose they say they think he is just a prophet, and then he tells them that he is really the great prophet Elijah, returned from the dead? Or suppose they say he's the Messiah, and he laughs and says, 'Don't be silly, I'm just a minor prophet'?

So, as usual, it is only Peter who has the courage of his convictions. He knows who he hopes Jesus is, and he doesn't care if saying it makes him look silly. His answer is right, of course, but he still looks silly.

Words are terribly important. Peter uses the word 'Messiah', and even though he has no idea at all what it means, the word is to become his whole vocation. As Jesus describes what Peter has actually said, the word, which has already shaped Jesus, is beginning to shape Peter too. He doesn't know it, but he has already accepted the definition that that word will give to his life – and death.

We don't usually believe that words have that kind of power. 'You are what you eat,' we say, but what about, 'You will be what you say'? What if our increasingly wordy and foul-mouthed world is actually choosing its destiny, with every word it utters? What if we are making ourselves vile, crude and debased, with no belief in the truth or the bindingness of words any more? As all our media sit increasingly lightly to the truth of what they report, they make truth something that we are no longer sure we can recognize. Distrust breeds. As more and more of us casually use disgusting language, we increasingly believe that others are the dirty and worthless things we say they are, and treat them accordingly.

That is what James suggests. The community to which he writes has a bad word problem. It is full of people who don't really think that words matter. You can say religious words without them affecting your lifestyle, and you can say horrible things and still call yourself a Christian, they think. But James says that your words are the things that guide your whole life. Whether you know it or not, you are judged by your words. Whether you know it or not, your words shape your future. James uses the illustration of a stream – it either gives good water or bad. It cannot do both. Words can contaminate the stream of life.

This concept of communication is so basic because God himself is the great communicator. The reading from Isaiah today pictures somebody whose ear is really attuned to the voice of God, so that he can 'sustain the weary with a word' (Isaiah 50.4). But those who constantly misuse words, and divorce them from their starting place in God, will eventually not recognize God's words – or his Word – at all. In Jesus, God's spoken word is lived and God's lived word is spoken, because in God there is never any separation between word and act. But the people around Jesus are reluctant to allow him to remake or recreate their speech. They try to make God's Word conform to their own language. When Peter speaks the word 'Messiah', he thinks he is defining Jesus. But really Jesus, the creative Word of God, is taking our words and remaking them into a language that we can again share with God. The process is painful and costly, as all three readings agree, but vital. Unless we give our language back to God, and allow him to retranslate all our ideas, we will continue to move further and further away from the truth that sets us free to communicate in God's language.

Proper 20

———— ∾ ————

Jeremiah 11.18–20
James 3.13—4.3, 7–8a
Mark 9.30–37

What an emotional roller-coaster ride the disciples are on by this stage of Jesus's ministry. Not that life with Jesus had ever been boring, exactly, but at least they had known what they were doing. Or they had thought they did, anyway. Whereas now, Jesus seems to be trying to undermine everything they thought they were following him for. They should have been on an emotional high. In Mark's Gospel, this episode is set immediately after the Transfiguration and the spectacular healing of a dramatically ill child. But instead of building on this, Jesus takes his disciples away and makes another attempt to explain his mission to them.

How can they possibly understand? After all, we who know the end of the story still do not really believe that Jesus is God's way with the world. We may say that we do, but we certainly don't act as though we do. Instead, we act just like the disciples. We nod wisely and bow our heads piously to the notion of the cross, and then we go away and argue about which of us is the most important. Like the disciples, we absolutely cannot see the connection between the power of God and the suffering and death of Jesus and, like them, we are afraid to ask because we don't want to know the answer. We want to get back to our interesting discussions about real power.

It is quite easy to see why the disciples, at this point in the story, might be arguing about which of them is the greatest. The three who witnessed the Transfiguration might well feel superior to the others, who had not only been left at the bottom of the mountain but had also failed to heal the sick boy while Peter, James and John were witnessing Jesus talking with Moses and Elijah. 'I expect we could have healed him,' you can hear Peter saying. 'But you don't pray any more than we do,' the others would protest.

In the middle of all these rivalries, and with the power that they have seen whizzing all around Jesus, which they long to be able to tap, how can they possibly pay attention to what Jesus is saying? How can they avoid being offended by the implication that some child they don't even know is more important to Jesus than they, who have followed him faithfully and given up so much to be his disciples?

Our society may pay lip-service to the importance of children, but they are still the ones on whom decisions are imposed, the ones who have to do as they are told. In Jesus's times, children would have had even less freedom and importance than we accord them. Jesus is deliberately choosing as his example someone with no status and no power. 'This is me,' he says, pointing to the anonymous child. 'If you want to be powerful, you won't be able to welcome someone like me.'

This is the part of Jesus's message that we – I – have most defended ourselves – myself – against. Instinctively we turn away from the belief that in this weakness and vulnerability, as in the rest of his life, Jesus is showing us the nature of God. In his healings, in his authoritative teaching, in his resurrection, we agree – there we see God's power. But in the form of a helpless child? Surely not! But the Christmas story tells us that that is precisely the route God chose to our salvation. So if we are called to be followers of Christ we, like the disciples, need to start trying to follow this path too. We might need to start by approaching unexpected people with caution and awe. The tramp, the cleaning lady, the checkout assistant, the bus conductor, the kind of people who are generally almost invisible in our lives – might they be the ones in whom we welcome Christ?

But if this is frightening and hard, it is also liberating and easy. We do not need to earn our place any more. We do not need to struggle to be 'best', to be important, to be greatest. We do not have to be at the centre of everything, frantically trying to prove that we are interesting. In the world of God's strange mercy, the minute we let go of this desperate obsession with ourselves, we are where we should be – beloved, chosen and free. No effort of ours can do it, but it doesn't need to. God has done all that needs doing, through the death and life of the Son. The Father welcomes us, helpless children, as though we were that other child, the Son. All we need to do is practise doing the same for others.

Proper 21

—— ∼ ——

Numbers 11.4–6, 10–16, 24–29
James 5.13–20
Mark 9.38–50

Moses has had enough of the people. He has led them out of slavery, and they have been saved and protected by God's strength throughout. They have seen the waters of the sea part just for them, they have seen water springing from the rock, just for them, and they have had food provided in the middle of the desert, simply because God is their protector. But still they whine. Now they don't like the kind of food God is giving them. They choose to forget that they were slaves in Egypt, and prefer instead to remember all the delicious meals that they had. They don't look around the barren, lifeless desert and praise God that they are alive at all. Instead they dream up menus, and blame Moses because they have tantalized themselves into a bad temper.

In other words, they are still living as slaves. They do not expect to make decisions or provisions for themselves. They look to Moses as to their former masters, without love or loyalty or thought of his feelings. They simply expect him to tell them what to do, and to provide for them, and when he fails, instead of taking any initiative themselves, they grumble.

So what happens now is the next stage in their liberation. They are physically no longer slaves, but mentally little has changed. Now God and Moses are going to make them take some responsibility for themselves. Now God takes some of the task he had given to Moses and shares it among the 70 elders of the people. From now on, they are to share Moses's responsibility for God's people, and begin to equip themselves for the freedom to which God has called them. With freedom goes power, but also responsibility. You cannot prophesy and heal one moment, sharing in the glorious power and purpose of God, and go off and sin the next, and pretend that the one is your responsibility and the other not.

110

Both Jesus and James make this connection. The two sections of today's Gospel reading don't seem immediately related, unless this is the key. In the first section, some people who are not immediately part of Jesus's circle have discovered the power of his name. They have accepted a share in the power of God, and Jesus says that a lot more goes with that, whether they know it or not. They have proved that through Jesus, God acts, and so they have become part of God's mission in Christ. They cannot step in when they want the buzz and excitement of power, and step out again when it comes to Jesus's teaching and his demands upon their whole lives. Either God does act in power through Jesus, or he doesn't. You can't have one bit without the other.

If these people who were healing in Jesus's name were doing it lightly, thinking they would just try it out for fun, then the second section of today's reading would have terrified them. In stepping into partnership with the power of God in Christ, they have stepped into one vision of the world and its purpose. And its demands are fierce and overriding. Nothing must ever tempt you to imagine a different course for yourself or the world. By exercising the power of God, you have become free, adult sharers in his mission, and have accepted responsibility for God's people.

These are sombre words for all those who try out God's power, intending to remain as slaves or children, intending always to run to someone else, or give up, or whine when things go wrong. If you accept God's protection and provision, you enmesh yourself immediately with God's people, with care for them and responsibility for them.

James speaks of the joyful power given to Christians in the name of Jesus. We have been given a share of God's saving and healing power, every one of us. This is not something to be reserved for heroes and saints, like Moses or Elijah, but is poured on us all, through Christ and the Spirit. But that immediately makes us all 'elders'. It's no longer somebody else's job to care for the sick, or to notice the lost, it is ours. But if this is burdensome, it also has its satisfactions. Perhaps it feels most irksome when we just sit and worry about it, instead of getting out there and doing it. James suggests that when you pray for the sick, search for the lost, live in close and truthful community with God's people, then you know what you are doing and why. You are sharing in God's great mission to bring his people out of the slavery of sin and death, and into his glorious kingdom.

Proper 22

—— ∾ ——

Genesis 2.18–24
Hebrews 1.14; 2.5–12
Mark 10.2–16

It is very tempting to go straight for the second half of the passage from Mark's Gospel set for today, and just speculate, if possible with some sentimentality, about what Jesus meant by 'theirs is the Kingdom of Heaven'. After all, the two halves of today's reading may not be very directly related – it may just be that the author thought, 'A saying about marriage and a saying about children go well together.' And it *is* endlessly fascinating to think about what particular quality children have that makes them such suitable inheritors of the Kingdom. But I think the two paragraphs may have more of a common theme than immediately emerges.

The question about marriage has obviously taken a lot of hard and cunning work to formulate and, interestingly, it seems to assume that the questioners did know that Jesus had rather a hard line about divorce. So they design a question to get Jesus into trouble, preferably with both religious and national institutions. Deuteronomy 24 assumes that divorce is bound to happen, and the Herod family were notorious for their broken marriages. (They try the same kind of tactics again in Mark 12. You can't help feeling that there was a minor industry in thinking up questions to trap Jesus.)

What Jesus does with the question is to open it up into a broader discussion of what scripture says about the purpose of creation. He does not say that Moses was wrong in allowing divorce, but he does say that the kind of technical discussions that focus on when divorce is acceptable and when it's not miss the point. He asks his questioners to look back to the Genesis creation story and remember that marriage is a gift from God. In all the glorious profusion of the new creation, with animals all around, still God sees that the creature God has made is lonely. It is very tempting to read this passage from Genesis 2 in terms of the slightly different narrative of

Genesis 1, and to add in the Christian belief in God as Trinity, and also to say that the creature on its own was not yet in God's image. To be in God's image, it needed to be distinct but united.

At the very least, Jesus is saying that human marriage is deep in the purposes of God, and that something of what God is trying to do in creating is lost in Moses's reluctant allowing of divorce in some circumstances.

To allow divorce because our hearts have become too hard to recognize God the Trinity at work in our relations is certainly not the only way in which we fail to understand why God created us. Jesus, who comes to ransom the world with his life because it can no longer find its own way back to God, surely knows this. But over and over again he tries to incite and excite people with a vision of the reality of God. Human religiousness is, instinctively, an attempt to harness God. What we long for from God is security and certainty. But the problem is that we look for that in places that are actually not God. Our security lies in the fact that we are utterly beloved by God, and that he wills for us to share his life, in his image. But we are constantly trying to bargain with God. 'If I do this, this and this, will you promise me a long and happy life?' What Jesus is saying is that negotiating about when God will allow us to break his image in us without minding too much is stupid. Of course we will break it, over and over again, as we crucified the Son. But if we can catch something of the vision of the nature of God and his purpose for us then the whole debate can be conducted on different grounds. It will no longer be our aim to justify ourselves in God's eyes, but to see how we can bring him our broken lives for healing.

And what does this have to do with the children? The disciples are treating the children as a problem. They are anxious to stop them from pestering Jesus. He is in the middle of a serious debate that may have ongoing consequences, the disciples themselves are uneasy about his teaching on divorce, and now these children come barging in. But Jesus sees the children as a gift. Is it too simplistic to say that they will inherit the Kingdom because it never occurs to them that they won't? They don't expect to earn it, but they have sensed that they give Jesus joy.

Proper 23

———— ◞ ————

Amos 5.6–7, 10–15
Hebrews 4.12–16
Mark 10.17–31

Is it just me, or are the readings actually getting harder at this time of year? Not only more difficult to understand, but also more sombre? Certainly, today's reading from Hebrews has taken large quantities of caffeine, and even so I'm not sure that I've got to the bottom of it. So if anyone out there has the key, I'd love to hear it.

The first half, Hebrews 4.12 and 13, is part of the argument that has been going on from the start of chapter 3. You can tell this because it is regularly punctuated by the phrase 'Today, if you hear his voice, do not harden your hearts' (cf. 3.7, 13, 15; 4.7). That is a quotation from Psalm 95, and in the Psalm it is clearly talking about the years of whining in the wilderness. It contains an underlying warning – that it is possible to see the wonderful works of God and yet not really believe in them as saving. How could the people whom God had liberated ever forget the parting of the waters, the pillar of cloud and of fire, the water and the manna? How could they ever believe that those were just passing phases in God's mercy, and convince themselves that God had lost interest and gone off and left them? But they did manage it, according to Deuteronomy and Numbers. Hebrews is arguing that if Moses was great and performed great deeds in God's name, then Jesus is even greater. We mustn't be tempted to lack of trust, like our forefathers.

So then, at the start of the passage set for today, the warning that has been fairly safely anchored in the past, in stories of our foolish ancestors, suddenly comes home. The rather rambling style of the previous chapter and a half, with its clauses, sub-clauses and quotations, suddenly flashes into life like the sword it describes.

What is this sharp, 'two-edged sword' that can pierce through things that you thought were completely welded together, and see through to a reality even you didn't know you were concealing

114

from yourself? The verses that follow make it clear that this living, active word is primarily Jesus, our great High Priest. But I think it also requires us to hear that in this particular context of perceptive, eagle-eyed judgement, it is Jesus speaking the word 'Today'. 'Today, if you will hear his voice' has been the refrain running through the last chapter and a half. It is a word requiring immediate response. It cannot take its time and talk about yesterday, and it cannot say, 'Hang on, let's see what happens tomorrow.' 'Today' is now or never.

And then the second half of this reading from Hebrews becomes less comforting, rather than more. Usually we read it as saying that Jesus understands our weaknesses and so he'll overlook them more easily. But notice it is also saying that, yes, he does understand our weaknesses, but he didn't give into them. The Israelites in the wilderness could just about argue that God didn't know what it was like to be hungry, thirsty and frightened, otherwise he might be a bit more understanding about their complaining. We have no such excuse.

It is interesting to see Jesus, the sharp two-edged sword, discerning exactly where the knife must go into the man who asks what he must do to inherit eternal life. Jesus looks at him and says 'Today' to the one thing the man cannot bear to do today. This is a man who is, by all standards, good, and he truly believed that there was no space between soul and spirit, joint and marrow where the sword of judgement could go in. But Jesus sees it, and says 'Today'. And the man goes away, shocked and grieving.

But notice that although Jesus has found the place of deceit in this man, he has done it with love (Mark 10.21). He does not let the disciples mock him, and he makes it clear that he knows how hard a thing he has asked. So much so that the disciples begin to panic about their own position. This man goes away by himself, either to accept or reject that 'Today'. But Hebrews suggests that we turn to the Word and ask for help. There is no point in trying to pretend in front of this living, active judge, but if 'Today' is the day of testing, it is also the day of mercy. There is no possibility of persuading the judge to let you in on your own merits, because for every one of us there was a 'Today' that we turned away from, and heard it as 'next week', 'next month', 'never'. So Hebrews recommends the bold approach – no concealment, relying only on the great High Priest.

Proper 24

——— ~ ———

Isaiah 53.4–12
Hebrews 5.1–10
Mark 10.35–45

There is an extraordinary consistency in what the New Testament tells us about the mission of Jesus Christ. At the heart of all the great biblical accounts of why the Son comes and how he saves us is the cross. No New Testament writer is tempted to underplay the suffering of Jesus and concentrate only on his teaching and his resurrection. Our human religious needs remain deeply suspicious of this strange way God has chosen to operate. We long to jump straight to the security and joy that we think God is supposed to be there to provide.

So James and John's request to Jesus is a natural one, and has rather better motives than many of ours. After all, they are taking it for granted that Jesus will, indeed, be reigning in glory one day soon; they are aware that there may well be some kind of a struggle and they are happy to play their part. They answer with confidence that, yes, of course they can share Jesus's cup and baptism. They'll fight by him with the best. But their main focus is the future, when all the nasty stuff will be over, and they will be on the winning side. Their concept of 'the winning side' has not been influenced at all by the conversation they have just had (Mark 10.32–35), in which Jesus tries to tell them what must happen to him.

The other disciples are indignant with James and John, so that Jesus has to sit them all down and tell them, in very simple language, what the values of a Christian disciple are to be. So what James, John and any other Christian disciple asks of Jesus, if we ask to share in his glory, is a life of service and suffering. However plain Jesus's language, you get the impression that the disciples didn't take it on board, but hurried on, saying, 'Yes, yes, but *after* that we get the reward, right?'

116

But according to Hebrews, the service and suffering *are* the reward. This is how God rewards the Son for his obedience, by putting him at the service of human beings for ever.

Hebrews takes us through this slowly and carefully, because it is a hard idea, and one we don't like the sound of. 'It's like this,' Hebrews says. 'You know what high priests do, don't you?'

A priest, according to Hebrews, is someone chosen – and the implication seems to be that the choice is made both by God and by us – to handle the relationship between God and people. The fact that he or she is chosen is the main qualification, the other one being that a priest is not essentially different from other human beings. Priestly work is done as much on the priest's own behalf as for others. So there is no particular merit in being chosen to be a mediator.

When Jesus takes on this role for us, Hebrews says, he knows that. He does not expect to be honoured for his priestly task, but simply responds in obedience to the call, as all human priests do. Jesus, like all priests, knows human need and human dependence upon God for salvation because he, like all others, knows weakness and human frailty. Although Hebrews is unequivocal about the fact that, unlike all other human beings, Jesus does not actually fall into sin (cf. 4.15), it is equally clear that he could have done. Such a possibility is not ruled out in advance by Jesus's divine and human nature, but is learned through struggle. Jesus learns the will of God, just like us, only better. So while ordinary human priesthood learns where God keeps the sticking plaster, Jesus's priesthood becomes the source of complete healing. It makes room not just for little drips of God's mercy but for the whole raging torrent of God's creative salvation. All the little devices which we have, up to now, thought of as 'priestly', devices that are to keep us more or less in God's favour without changing too much, all of these now become obsolete. 'Priesthood' tries to bring God and humanity close enough to come to some kind of understanding, but Jesus brings God and humanity together in dynamic unity, so that God's salvation can never be misunderstood again. This is Jesus's 'reward' – his 'priesthood', learned in suffering and obedience, will last for ever. Perhaps that was not the kind of glory that James and John had in mind, but through the eternal priesthood of Christ we too can offer the fruits of his priesthood to a hungry world.

Proper 25

—— ◇ ——

Jeremiah 31.7–9
Hebrews 7.23–28
Mark 10.46–52

Some theologies sound a bit vague about what happens to Jesus after the resurrection. His work is completed, once for all, on the cross, he is vindicated by the Father through the resurrection, and that's that. Then, depending on your point of view, either the Holy Spirit takes over or the Bible does or else human morality does, with pious references to the Jesus who is now conveniently not there to be checked with. (I am, of course, exaggerating, but bear with me.) The Holy Spirit knows about the cross but that's all in the past now, and the present job of believers is to tap into the power that the Holy Spirit has to offer, and not to talk about that nasty old cross too much. The Bible, too, knows about the cross, since it tells about it at great length, but its present role is to give to believers a certainty and power that is not at all unlike that delivered by the Holy Spirit, though without the choruses. Human morality expects our own will-power to deliver the goods. It talks about the cross as something that really could have been and should be avoided, if only we will follow Jesus's example and be thoroughly nice to each other and non-judgemental.

As I said, I am exaggerating and caricaturing. No one I know actually espouses any of the post-Jesus theologies I have just outlined, though they do sometimes come quite close. But the basic thing that all these caricatures share, which is an ever-present danger, is to forget, imaginatively, that Jesus is not an aberration, but our only real clue to the nature of God. All these unreal theologies assume that Jesus is basically in the past. They may pay theoretical lip-service to him, but their view of God has not been fundamentally altered by the life, death and resurrection of Jesus. Fundamentally, we continue to believe that God is there to deliver what we need.

And, of course, that is true. God is indeed there to deliver what we need. The only problem is that we don't know what that is, and we constantly confuse what we want with what we need.

Does the blind man in Mark 10 *need* to see? Many blind people would argue not. Being blind is a way of life, different from that of the sighted, but not worse, certainly not in religious terms. What is it that Bartimaeus *needs* from this encounter with Jesus? Does it perhaps lie in that last verse of today's reading? Jesus tells him that his faith has made him well, and Bartimaeus responds by following Jesus. The need Jesus sees in him is his need to be a faithful disciple, a need that he doesn't believe he can ever fulfil and hasn't even voiced to himself. He is lucky enough to find that what he wants and what he needs coincide. The thing he is prepared to admit that he wants – his sight – leads into what he needs, which is a certainty that he is worthy and able to follow Jesus, that his faith is up to the task. Actually, there was no particular reason why he shouldn't, as a blind person, be a disciple, but he couldn't believe that. Jesus gives him charge of his own choices, and he instantly chooses to follow.

Hebrews argues that that discernment, which we see over and over again in the earthly Jesus, continues to be his vocation for ever, as it always was and always will be. Hebrews calls it 'priesthood', and links it for ever to our salvation. Jesus's work, completed once for all on the cross, makes him the means by which we can approach God in our need for ever. Just as the earthly Jesus looked at people, called them and challenged them to recognize their true need, so Jesus our intercessor continues to do. This is not passive passing-on of superficial requests to a rather bored God, but a genuine gateway between what we think we need and what God calls us into.

'It is fitting', Hebrews 7.26 says, 'that we should have such a high priest.' Why is it? What is so fitting about this Son of God, who has done what none of us, priest or otherwise, is capable of doing, and offered perfect obedience to God in our human form? What is fitting about that? It is fitting because that is what we need. We need to be what we are made to be and called to be, which is God's children, sharing the love of Father, Son and Holy Spirit. 'What do you want?' Jesus asks, and keeps asking, until we see that what we need is to follow him.

Sundays Before Advent

The Fourth Sunday Before Advent

———— ∽ ————

Deuteronomy 6.1–9
Hebrews 9.11–14
Mark 12.28–34

Person A:

Do I love God? Well, why should I? What's God ever done for me? I've worked hard all my life and nobody's ever given me a thing. There are people out there born with everything they'll ever need – they can love God if they like. They can sing songs to God as though he was their boyfriend, and weep with joy at how good it makes them feel. God's for people who don't need to fight and cheat just to stay alive. Is it right that some people never have to do a hand's turn and are surrounded by people who love and admire them, while some of us can barely keep ourselves alive by working twenty-four hours a day, and everybody despises us? The law's there, like God, to protect the people who have.

I was doing quite a good day's work, picking pockets in the crowd the other day. They were all gathered round this man, Jesus. I've made quite a good living out of him, because he draws a crowd wherever he goes, and they forget to keep their hands on their wallets. Well, I nearly got caught because I got too interested in the discussion. They were talking about the law and about loving God, and they seemed to think that if you love God and you love your neighbour, then you've kept the law. I must remember that one, next time I'm up in front of the magistrate. So I said to this snooty-looking woman, standing listening to them, 'Give us a kiss, show how much you love God.' She gave me a really dirty look, but some people laughed. I felt quite pleased with myself, till I realized I'd made them turn and look at me, which isn't professional, for a pickpocket. I had to scarper. But as I walked home, I got quite angry, thinking about the discussion. When people start giving me their wallets before I take them, I'll believe they love God and their neighbours, not before. I can't start being all soppy to other people first, or what would I live on?

Person B:

I was just doing the shopping when I saw a crowd of people standing round Jesus, listening to him talking to some scribe. I stopped to have a look. I've heard Jesus before, and although I don't agree with him, I find him quite interesting. I mean, he was saying today that all you have to do is love God and love your neighbour and you can forget the rest. Well, obviously that's nonsense, isn't it? I mean, naturally I love God, though I find it a bit embarrassing to have such words bandied about. After all, that's rather personal, isn't it? I know I've always tried to do what is right, and have often consulted my minister about exactly what is and what isn't allowed on the Sabbath. But surely that's far more important than all this nonsense about 'love'? And I hope I've always been a good neighbour. I keep my house and yard clean and quiet, and I give charity to the real poor. Obviously, you can't let yourself be put upon and exploited by people, like that nasty, dirty chap who tried to get a laugh by asking me to kiss him, to show my love. People like that can't be loved, they don't understand the meaning of the word. No, I'm confident that I've done my best by living a decent life and keeping myself to myself. All that nonsense about love is just a way of ducking out of our responsibilities.

Person C:

I don't know what made me agree with Jesus. I think I just felt he could do with a kind word. People had been questioning him and tricking him and arguing with him all day. When I asked my question about what's the most important commandment, I could see he thought I was doing the same. But I wanted everyone listening to think about what they were doing. They weren't trying to please God, they were just trying to make Jesus's life a misery. His answer was exactly right. From what I've heard, that's just what he tries to do. He tries to get people to see God as a loving God, worth loving in return, and he tries to get people to treat each other with forgiveness and care. I don't know why that makes them all so mad. But he looked so tired, that I just said, 'You *are* right, you know. Don't ever let them make you doubt it.' I'll never forget how he looked at me. Such gratitude, for such a small thing. I felt really warmed, as though God's sun had suddenly shone right on me.

The Third Sunday Before Advent

——— ∾ ———

Jonah 3.1–5, 10
Hebrews 9.24–28
Mark 1.14–20

Hebrews is convinced that the work of Jesus is completed in the cross. And not just the work of the Son of God, but the whole providential work of God in creating us in the first place. The cross of Christ is 'the end of the age'. Nothing more can ever happen that will change what God has done for us, or replace our triumphant and suffering judge with some other. Remember how this letter starts, like the Gospel of John, with the big picture. Before all else, the Son is with the Father in creating and sustaining the world. He is 'the reflection of God's glory and the exact imprint of God's very being' (Hebrews 1.3). It is vital to remember this setting in all that Hebrews goes on to say about the High Priesthood of Christ. Christ's dealings with us are part of God's eternal creative design, and the glory and imprint of God is as much to be found in the cross as in the worship of the angels. The cross of Christ is the denouement, it is where God intended to lay bare the plot. Any careful reader, Hebrews argues, could see all the clues and be prepared. There is a great urgency in Hebrews, as the author pulls images and quotations from the Jewish scriptures and from the religious practices that his readers would have been familiar with, and tries to show that each is a hint, a shadow, a preparation, however poor, for God's great work of salvation.

The same kind of urgency rings through today's other readings. Jonah gets up, obedient at last, to walk across the great city of Nineveh and warn of God's judgement; and Simon, Andrew, James and John throw in their lot with Jesus, little knowing what consequences it will have.

There is, of course, a huge difference in what Jonah proclaims and in what makes the disciples follow Jesus. Jonah is proclaiming judgement. 'It's too late!' he shouts, 'You are going to pay for your wicked lives. You and your city will be destroyed!' You can hear both the relish and the uncertainty in what he was saying. This is what he hopes will happen, but will it?

Jesus, on the other hand, is offering an alternative. Jonah wants people to suffer for their sins, but Jesus apparently wants them to chánge and hear 'good news'. According to Mark, there are two elements to this good news – the general and the particular. The general is that 'the Kingdom of God has come near', and the particular is that specific invitation to the disciples, 'You, come and make it come near for others.'

In a way, Jonah too is saying, 'The Kingdom of God has come near', but for him God's rule is punitive, and there is nothing that anyone can do about it. Much to his annoyance, he turns out to be wrong in that. God, the King, makes room for the second, specific invitation that Jonah leaves out. 'Make a difference,' God adds, in effect. He leaves room, as Jonah doesn't, for the people of Nineveh to change.

Hebrews is not saying 'The kingdom of God has come near.' It is saying, 'God is ruling, now.' But although completeness and finality are central to Hebrews' theology of the cross, it is clear that there is still an expectation that we will join in – that like the people of Nineveh, we will repent, and like the disciples, we will become fishers of men.

But if the work of God is done and completed in Christ, why must we still do it? I suppose the answer lies partly in Jonah. We still do not, in our heart of hearts, think that God knows what he is up to, and so we are still in the process of repentance. Jonah longs for God to judge with his own standards of judgement, which are perfectly good and learned from good religious sources. But he wants God to be just and to preserve his honour and greatness – not just Jonah's but God's own. That's what we just do not understand, that God's honour and greatness lie in his total faithfulness to what he has always been and always will be – the God who made us for himself. Jonah would have been horrified at the idea of God dying on the cross, and Jonah has never been alone in this. But if God is really the maker and ruler of the world, then he alone knows how it works. This is how it is done, Hebrews says. Nothing else works, only this. It is not God who has to change until he learns to leave out the cross. We have to repent until we hear it as good news.

The Second Sunday Before Advent

———— ~ ————

Daniel 12.1–3
Hebrews 10.11–25
Mark 13.1–8

All of today's readings are set against the background of a disinte-grating world, and all see that as something joyful. Daniel and Mark seem to be talking about the future, though there is no indi-cation about how far away that future is – certainly close enough to impact on present behaviour. Pretty well every historical era has read the descriptions in Daniel and Mark as closely describing its own circumstances, and pretty well every era has then given in to the temptation of second-guessing God's judgement. But that is pre-cisely what all the passages deplore.

Daniel speaks of the time of deliverance as accompanied by 'anguish' – such a strong word, yet certainly describing the lives of many in our time, living and dying with poverty, war, disease, tor-ture and manifold injustices. To long for a prince and protector is natural, just as natural as it is to assume that the role of such a person is to condemn our enemies, those who have made our lives such anguish. But what Daniel longs for is a time when wisdom and righteousness will be visible. With utter profundity and simplicity, he identifies the missing ingredients that make it possible for us to inflict anguish on one another. We do not recognize wisdom and righteousness. They do not blaze across our skies. People argue with one another about what is right or wise, and bury wisdom and righteousness deeper and deeper underground. Daniel's vision of deliverance is of a time when wisdom and righteousness are the lights in the sky, by which we make our every movement, wholly clear and unarguable. Under those lights, we will not need to con-demn or praise one another, because the light itself will make the judgement clear. Daniel does not long primarily to be justified and to see his enemies suffer, but he longs to know what is right and good.

What the disciples long to know is 'When?' But they don't get an answer. If you notice, the disciples very often have their eyes fixed on the future. They are aware that they are part of something important, but a lot of the time it doesn't feel important in a way that they can identify. Now, finally, Jesus seems to be talking about revolutionary change. 'At last,' they say. 'So, when's it going to happen, and how can we be sure that we're ready for action when the time comes? What will the signal be?'

Frustratingly, Jesus simply describes to them the world that they, and we, have to live in. And as in Daniel's time of anguish, what is missing is any way of being really sure where the truth lies. Many different factions will be claiming to represent the work of Christ, and every side in every conflict will be sure that right is on their side only. Simple realism suggests that Christian disciples will not always get it right. Some of us will be 'led astray', and we will not always be able to resist being alarmed. You have to read the rest of chapter 13 to find out what strategy Jesus recommends, but I will give you a clue. It is a really difficult one, and it involves an alert restfulness and concentration on the figure of Jesus that has certainly not always characterized the Christian Church, and generally doesn't today. We are still much more prone to shout 'When? When will you come, Lord, and show the rest of the world that I'm right and they're wrong?'

But Hebrews recommends the exact same strategy as Mark. Concentrate on Jesus. In the work of Jesus, everything is already accomplished. We may not always see and feel that, caught as we are in the middle of the anguish, and Hebrews does not want immunity from reality for us. It says we must step into Jesus, into the suffering, torn flesh that is our hope and our reality. The assurance that we have in Christ Jesus is not an assurance of protection or tranquillity, nor even a fail-safe method for discerning wisdom and righteousness, but just a total dependence upon the faithfulness of God. The judgement is not ours. It will not fail if we are not at the centre of it. The work we are given is almost insultingly small, and yet we are quite incapable of doing even that much. Hebrews says we have to learn to live together, even with those we have not chosen, in love and kindness, 'encouraging one another' (Hebrews 10.24–5). We would much rather charge around, wielding judgement in God's name, but remember that in Mark, Jesus says that is just what imposters do. Christian disciples work at living together in Christ.

Christ the King

—— $\approx$ ——

Daniel 7.9–10, 13, 14
Revelation 1.4b–8
John 18.33–37

Philip Pullman's brilliant *His Dark Materials* trilogy ends with the words 'and then we'll build . . . The republic of heaven.' This is the vision that Lyra holds out to us after all she has learned and suffered – that human beings must and can learn to live wisely and unselfishly and build worlds that help others to do the same. There is no place for God in Lyra's picture, because a concept of God would, according to what Lyra has seen, automatically undermine her vision of a human republic of heaven. Throughout the trilogy it has become clear that 'God' is a cipher that power-hungry people use to justify violence and to impose their will on others. 'God's' followers never have to give an account of themselves, or answer to others for their actions, because they are all justified in the name of their service to God, the ruler.

This is a critique that all Christians should take seriously. Do we, indeed, use the notion of God's rule actually to impose our own? Do we demand, in God's name, the power and respect that we long for ourselves? Do we impose our understanding of the world on those weaker than ourselves, and tell them that it is God's understanding? I'm afraid that in the past the answer has often been 'Yes', and still is. The readings for today focus on Christ as King, and they are a severe challenge, to Christians first and foremost. They suggest that this most vital and central fact about Jesus, whom we believe to be 'the image of the invisible God', is one that we have not taken into our hearts and minds at all. It is the most counter-intuitive thing about the Christian concept of God, and our systems of belief and behaviour and organization barely reflect it in any way.

The reading from Daniel starts off with a picture of power that is reasonably in line with our undisturbed non-Christian understanding of power. Perhaps, nowadays, we would prefer our ruler not to be called 'the Ancient One', but at least there are thrones and fire and innumerable bowing servants. But then what happens? An ordinary human being, who looks very like the rest of us, comes to the awesome throne, and instantly the fire and throne and bowing crowds fade, and we wait to see how they will be manifested in this unprepossessing human figure.

So then the reading from Revelation takes up the story. Now we have seen how this human figure was to exercise dominion. He came to love us and die for us. His dying, Revelation says, has made us free people, who can exercise our freedom to act as he did, in service.

The reading from St John's Gospel makes the point even more graphically, because it has two pictures of power face to face. Pilate's power we recognize. Pilate exercises power over these squabbling people, whom he really can't be bothered to understand. They have brought a man to him and, although Pilate knows the charges are trumped up, that is not his concern. He goes straight to the only point that is of interest to him: 'Are you challenging my power?' And he reads Jesus's answer – rightly – as a 'Yes'. He is too impatient to hear exactly why, but he is surely right to pounce on that central word, 'King'. If Jesus is King, then Pilate is not.

If Pilate had really listened to the nuances of what Jesus was saying, would it have changed his mind? Jesus's kingship, after all, has left Pilate's kind apparently largely untouched. Jesus himself points out that his followers are hardly acting like revolutionaries, bent on setting up their own king. But when Jesus offers to explain to Pilate exactly what his kingship is, Pilate doesn't care. He is obsessed with the one word, 'King'. To him, it means only one thing, and that is a thing that he longs for and would commit any perjury and injustice for – power.

But what Jesus is offering as a description of his own kingship is truth – reality, you might say. Revelation calls it 'the Alpha and Omega, who was and is and is to come'. If the actual reality of the world, from its creation to its end, is like Jesus, then this strange human obsession with power is an aberration. It has no ability to create, to redeem or to sanctify. Jesus's challenge to Pilate's kind of power is too slow and subtle for many of us, who long to use the weapons of worldly power to force victory for God. But if Jesus is the truth, then any other way is falsehood, and will fail. Reality, as it was and is and is to come, is shaped by a different kingship.

The Society for Promoting Christian Knowledge (SPCK) was founded in 1698. Its mission statement is:

To promote Christian knowledge by

- **Communicating the Christian faith in its rich diversity;**
- **Helping people to understand the Christian faith and to develop their personal faith; and**
- **Equipping Christians for mission and ministry.**

SPCK Worldwide serves the Church through Christian literature and communication projects in over 100 countries, and provides books for those training for ministry in many parts of the developing world. This worldwide service depends upon the generosity of others and all gifts are spent wholly on ministry programmes, without deductions.

SPCK Bookshops support the life of the Christian community by making available a full range of Christian literature and other resources, providing support for those training for ministry, and assisting bookstalls and book agents throughout the UK.

SPCK Publishing produces Christian books and resources, covering a wide range of inspirational, pastoral, practical and academic subjects. Authors are drawn from many different Christian traditions, and publications aim to meet the needs of a wide variety of readers in the UK and throughout the world.

The Society does not necessarily endorse the individual views contained in its publications, but hopes they stimulate readers to think about and further develop their Christian faith.

For further information about the Society, visit our website at *www.spck.org.uk* or write to:
SPCK, 36 Causton Street,
London SW1P 4ST, United Kingdom.